CREATURES
OF THE
NIGHT

✳ ✳ ✳ ✳ ✳

THE ROCKY HORROR EXPERIENCE

BY SAL PIRO

FOREWORD BY RICHARD O'BRIEN

Binary
PUBLICATIONS

CREATURES OF THE NIGHT
The Rocky Horror Experience

By Sal Piro

Edited by Meryline Scneider
Front Cover photo credit: John Jay.
Special thanks to Judy Verdino

NOTE: This is a re-presentation of the original book released from Stabur Press in 1990. So, many of the references are to the 15th Anniversary which was occurring at that time.

CONTENTS

Foreword

I met Sal Piro way back in 19 mmmm tee ummmm, he was younger then as was I, I'm still younger but Sal, like the rest of the 'HUMAN' race is over-taking me like there's no tomorrow, maybe he and they know something that we 'visitors don't, like, what's the secret of Vanna White's success? and why don't you ever see a yellow rose in Texas? to raise just two of the questions that have been perplexing all thinking beings where ever they might originate from.

Sal has bounced (I use the word advisedly) into the lives of many ROCKY HORROR fans and has given them a real good time. He is the High priest of the church of liberation, turn up for a weekly service, and he will give communion, read the service and shake it 'till the walls come tumblin' down.

He's a native New Yorker, a writer, a producer, director and related to a lottery winner. I like him.

If I was asked to sum up Sal, I'd say, two legs, two arms, a body, neck and head...-okay, so I forgot the hands and feet, I'm only alien.

This book will make an ideal Christmas, Birthday, Easter, New Year, Anniversary, Valentine, Passover, Show opening, Show closing, Fun and informative gift for you and all the family. Amaze your friends! Be the first one on your block to possess a copy! With this book you can strengthen your thighs, increase your sex appeal and broaden your mind, not bad for the mere pittance it cost, is it?

Don't argue with me.

Happy reading,

Richard O'Brien

DEDICATION

To:

LARRY FOR THE START

DORI FOR THE SPIRIT

ALEX FOR THE SMARTS

ADAM FOR SUSTAINING

RICHARD, MICHAEL & LOU FOR THE SUPPORT

AND

LILLIAS FOR EVERYTHING

INTRODUCTION

In early 1973, Richard O'Brien's musical THE ROCKY HORROR SHOW starring Tim Curry opened at the Royal Court Theater Upstairs for a five-week experimental run. It was an immediate success and moved to the larger King's Road Theater. The show won all sorts of awards, including "Best Musical," given by the London Evening Standard. It later moved to the even larger Comedy Theater where it had an incredible seven-year run.

Early in its British run, THE ROCKY HORROR SHOW was seen by rock and roll impresario Lou Adler who purchased the American rights to the play. In 1974 the show had its American premier at the Roxy Theater in Los Angeles. This production, which again starred Tim Curry, had a successful stint of over a year. The play was not so fortunate in its New York run on Broadway, where it ran at the Belasco Theater for only forty-nine performances in April of 1975.

Meanwhile, the movie was produced as a joint venture by Lou Adler and the show's British producer Michael White. THE ROCKY HORROR PICTURE SHOW starred Tim Curry and author Richard O'Brien, recreating their original roles of Dr. Frank-N-Furter and Riff Raff. American film star Susan Sarandon was cast as Janet, the film's heroine, and Broadway actor Barry Bostwick was cast as nerd hero Brad Majors. Rock singer Meatloaf was cast as Eddie, the role he had played in the Roxy production.

The film had its American premier in late September of 1975 in Los Angeles and a few key test cities. With the exception of Los Angeles (where the play was a success), the movie was considered a failure, not given a major release and promptly shelved. Then, on April Fools' Day 1976, a young executive at Twentieth Century Fox persuaded the Waverly Theater in New York City to replace their midnight show with THE ROCKY HORROR PICTURE SHOW. Ironically, the city that rejected the play welcomed this movie with open arms. A loyal group of fans came to see the film over and over again. They so loved the movie that they began to spontaneously participate with it by:

- chanting a litany of responses and directions to the screen
- wearing the makeup and costumes of the film's characters
- utilizing props to enhance the atmosphere of the film in the theater
- ultimately performing the film in the audience and in front of the screen simultaneously to its actions

This audience participation began to spread as the movie was booked at theaters throughout the country in midnight showings. Since then, THE ROCKY HORROR PICTURE SHOW has become the number one cult and midnight movie of all time. And the audience participation madness has spread throughout the world.

I am fortunate to be one of those people who became a part of the RHPS movement. This is my story and the story of all the ROCKY fans who celebrate Halloween all year long, who give themselves over to "absolute pleasure" and who devote themselves to one of the most special films ever made.

Sal Piro

CREATURES

OF THE

NIGHT

* * * * *

THE
ROCKY HORROR
EXPERIENCE

he first time I saw the ROCKY HORROR PICTURE SHOW was at the Waverly Theater in Greenwich Village, late in January, 1977. ROCKY had already been playing there for nine months, but I did not know much about it. Some girls I met at a party who'd seen the show on Broadway told me of it, and so did my friend, Michael Kester. He had seen the film nineteen times and could not stop raving about it.

It didn't seem unusual to me that Michael had seen a movie so often. After all, I had seen many of my favorites more that twenty times. But that Michael, with whom I shared a passion for music and film, had seen the RHPS so very many times impressed me, and I began to be curious about it. I still never dreamed that I would go to this film — any film — more than 1300 times.

The American premiere of the ROCKY HORROR PICTURE SHOW was at the Westwood Theater in Los Angeles, in late September of 1975. Even though it played in a few test market cities, the film was considered a failure and did not get a wide release and was shelved.

Then, on April Fools' Day, 1976, Tim Deegan, a young advertising executive at 20th Century Fox, persuaded Bill Quigley of the Walter Reade Organization to replace the midnight show at the Waverly Theater with the ROCKY HORROR PICTURE SHOW. The Waverly had already been a mecca for midnight movies and had had two very successful runs, of El Topo and Night Of The Living Dead. The manager of the Waverly, Denise Borden, was fascinated with the film and she began her own personal hype campaign, with photos in the box office window and a theater telephone recording that stated, "This is a film not to be missed."

Denise would play the record album of the RHPS sound track before the showing of the film to warm up the audience, and a party atmosphere was generated as a result. The audiences naturally began to respond, by booing the villain and cheering the heroes, and as Jim Sharman, the director of ROCKY HORROR, has said, "With typical Saturday morning serial stuff." This spawned a whole group of regulars who weekly reserved the same seats in the first row of the balcony. These pioneers of audience participation from the balcony included two young ladies named Amy and Theresa; Bill O'Brien, the first person to dress as *Dr. Frank-N-Furter*; Lori Davis, who wrote the Ten Commandments of ROCKY HORROR; and Louis Farese, a kindergarten teacher from Staten Island.

On Labor Day weekend of 1976, Louis felt compelled to speak to the screen. He is credited as the first person to yell lines at the movie. His earliest lines were: "Buy an umbrella, you cheap bitch!"— to *Janet* walking in the rain, and "How strange was it?" — to *the criminologist's* initial speech. (Louis called this "counterpoint dialogue.") Then, in late September, as they sought a preview of Halloween, a few people came dressed as characters from the movie. Later, on Halloween, there was a costume party with many people dressing as the characters.

RUNNING JOKES

The criminologist who wears a high collar and has a short neck is constantly derided with "This man has no neck" or appropriate "no-neck" lines.

☆ ☆

Brad is always greeted with a chorus of "asshole" as a tribute to his nerd status..

☆ ☆

Janet is likewise greeted with a chorus of "slut" when she appears.

Louis Farese, credited with being the first person to talk back to the screen.

Bill O'Brien and a few of the regulars began to lip-sync the record that is played before the movie in front of the audience. This was spontaneous and it developed into a mini-floor show before the movie. Audience response was tremendous.

Around the first of the year, in unexplained circumstances, the floor show moved to the New Yorker Theater, on Manhattan's Upper West Side. The ROCKY HORROR PICTURE SHOW had been playing there since June, but was not doing very well. The theater was larger, with a stage, which may have partly motivated the move. The audience there, however, displayed no real interest in the floor show; so it was eliminated and the regulars returned to the Waverly.

I was a former seminarian who spent three years teaching theology and directing school plays in Catholic high schools in New Jersey. I was laid off from my teaching job in June of 1976 and spent that summer being a drama director in an all-girls camp in the Berkshire Mountains. When I returned, I decided I would move into New York City and try my hand as a "starving actor." I took a job waiting tables and got some roles in off-Broadway shows. Then I went to see ROCKY HORROR.

It was a cold snowy night when four friends and I found ourselves outside the Waverly waiting for over an hour before we were allowed in to see the show. One of these friends was Marc Shaiman who went on to become musical director for Bette Midler, Billy Crystal and other stars. He sat next to me for the next seventy-five times I saw the RHPS. Both of us contributed ad-lib lines that became part of the whole spectacular "happening."

What we saw at our virgin[1] viewing was the now famous pre-

---

1. VIRGIN / v r-jan/ (n) — anybody who has never seen the ROCKY HORROR PICTURE SHOW, (virgin viewing — seeing RHPS for the first time).

movie floor show. Anticipating what was to come, I became more and more excited. I found the energy and enthusiasm generated in the theater catching. The film started. The lips . . . the Time Warp . . . *Frank's* fabulous entrance . . . image followed image, and the impact on me was tremendous. I began living the movie as it unreeled.

Waiting in line in the early days of The Waverly.

The first time I heard Louis Farese's voice speaking back to the screen, it was funny and I was delighted. Suddenly I was ten years old again, going with my mother to see Snow White and the Three Stooges. I remember that just as Snow White was about to bite into the poisonous apple, a voice from somewhere in the movie theater warned audibly, "You'll be sooorry!" The whole theater rocked with laughter. As the film continued, I wanted to shout out something clever too, but I didn't have the nerve.

I remembered Zacherly, the ghoulish host of TV's Creature Features, who interrupted scenes from old "B" horror films with zany remarks and wisecracks. It always broke me up. (Oh, what he did to The Attack Of The Giant Crab Monsters!) Eventually, I began ad-libbing a remark or two during other movies myself. Sometimes people laughed, but more often I heard, "Quiet!" from annoyed members of the audience or my embarrassed friends.

But now, thanks to Louis and friends, it was all right to talk back to the screen. By the time I had watched RHPS twice, I knew by heart the places to yell lines and how to time them. By my third viewing, I was ready to try my hand at an original line. When *Frank* asked, "Whatever happened to Fay Wray?" I answered, "She went apeshit!" — exactly what the audience did when they heard me. This was the first of dozens of lines that I created. Some of them were forgotten, but plenty of them are still shouted out in theaters across the country today.

Pleased with this quick success, Marc and I developed a regular litany connecting the audience to what was happening on the screen. Marc's favorite line was his answer to *Magenta's*, "Master! Dinner is prepared." "And we helped," was Marc's contribution. My own favorite, and one of the most popular in the New York area, occurs before, "Toucha Toucha Touch Me." When *Rocky* touches *Janet's* hand, the audience asks: "Hey *Janet*, you wanna fuck?" (*Janet* turns her head.) "Think about it," they shout, as she smiles from the screen.

I not only invented lines; if I heard someone else's line and liked it, I kept it alive by integrating it with the rest of the litany. This is how the show "went public," people inventing lines and using the lines of others. An individual would yell a line; others would pick it up; then a whole group and eventually the entire audience would shout out the line together. Today, "old-timers" say that sometimes they miss the spontaneity of a single person creating a new line; they feel that the impact is lost when over a hundred people yell out lines, usually out of sync, at that. I don't agree. I feel everyone reacting together to the film is part of the charm — ROCKY fans as a community chanting and reacting to their film with love and affection.

Alan Riis was another who excelled at originating lines. Alan was a college student from Brooklyn, active in local and civic organizations. He was first exposed to RHPS in May of 1977, brought to the theater by his friend, Laura Stein. Alan was crazy about Dr. Demento, a disc jockey specializing in bizarre humor. Once Alan sent him a 700-signature petition, asking that he play "Time Warp." Since then, Dr. Demento has featured ROCKY HORROR music on his syndicated show a lot. The RHPS was clearly a great outlet for Alan's talents and imagination. His most famous line is the one that starts off the audience participation with: "And God said, 'Let there be lips!'" just as the movie begins with an image of a huge pair of lips.

Alan and Ed Bordenka were responsible for bringing many of the Waverly innovations to other theaters in the New York area. While Ed didn't invent many lines himself, his devotion to the film was, and is, incredible. He has seen it over 500 times in many different theaters and he says each time is as good as the first. He and Alan also traveled outside city limits to many of the other ROCKY HORROR theater showings that sprang up in mid-1977. At each of them, Ed's extremely loud voice spread the lines that had originated at the Waverly. This caused problems sometimes, because regulars at those other theaters, when they heard Ed and Alan, believed the lines were being created right then and there. And you can imagine the arguments that we Waverly regulars have had in other theaters when we've tried to convince other devotees that most of their lines had originated with us!

Props

Meanwhile, back in the first-row balcony, creativity had not yet been exhausted. The logical step after talking in unison with, and then at, the screen was actual physical participation in the film — through the use of props. The first ones used were rice and cards. Amy Lazarus says it was sometime in April of 1977, about a year after RHPS opened at the Waverly, that she and her friend Theresa ripped paper up and threw it, like confetti, during the wedding scene. The following night, Bill and Lori handed out rice for people along their row to throw. I was not there that particular weekend, but I was the next, when regulars picked up the cue and threw rice during the wedding scene. It caused pandemonium in the theater. At the moment when I, a neophyte of only twenty viewings, was pelted with rice, I realized the possibilities ahead. Something really new, really exciting was happening and I felt part of it.

Lori Davis was the first to throw playing cards during the song, "I'm Going Home," while *Frank* is singing "cards for sorrow, cards for pain." She explained why she did it: "The Master said cards — I bring the cards." Lori made a confession, too. For a while she had kept her weight down to 98 pounds because of a line in the "Charles Atlas" song, but had to give it up when it made her ill. Now people throw playing cards, greeting cards, computer cards and pieces of cardboard marked "sorrow" and "pain."

Candles were the next important prop. Louis Farese tells how one night he was handed a candle by Bill and Lori, for the "candle ceremony." During "Light in the Frankenstein Place," everyone in the front row balcony stood up, a lit candle in their hand. No one intended this to be a regular part of the routine, but a group from the orchestra took up the practice and it continued.

During the rain scene one night, Alan Riis, who sat in the orchestra, put a newspaper on his head as *Janet* does to protect her head. In spite of the mockery this caused, Alan continued to do it for three weekends, determined the idea would catch on.

Eighteen months later, I sat in a theater where at least three-quarters of the audience wore newspaper hats on their heads. I smiled and was glad at the tribute to Alan's stubbornness. Today, newspapers are one of the most popular props because they are cheap and easy to find. Even during a newspaper

Teresa and Amy, early ROCKY pioneers.   Photo: Fredda Tone

Candle ceremony at The Waverly before the ban.

Photo: Stephanie Saia

*Newspapers and candles
— "There's A Light" at
The Waverly.*

strike, ROCKY HORROR fans always managed. To enhance this scene, people began to use water pistols to simulate rain. (Thank goodness we had newspapers on our head!)

From then on, any obvious prop was used. Here is a list of the most important ones, used by any well-equipped ROCKY HORROR fan, and along with Rice, Cards and Newspapers, all are essential to the constant viewer:

Confetti: At the end of the "Charles Atlas" song reprise, the Transylvanians throw confetti as *Rocky* and *Frank* head toward the bedroom. The audience throws it too.

Rubber Gloves: During and after the creation speech, *Frank* snaps his rubber gloves three times. Later, *Magenta* pulls them off his hands. The audience snaps rubber gloves in sync, creating a fantastic sound effect.

Party Hats: At the dinner table, when *Frank* puts on a party hat, those in the audience don theirs.

Noisemakers: At the end of the creation speech, the Transylvanians respond with cheers and noisemakers. So do those watching.

Toast: When *Frank* proposes a toast at dinner, members of the audience throw toast in the air. This is one of the most popular routines. I'm just glad that no one has thought of putting butter and jam on the toast; things could get sticky!

Toilet Paper: When *Dr. Scott* enters the lab, *Brad* cries out "Great Scott!" The audience hurls rolls of toilet paper into the air (preferably Scott's).

<u>Water Pistols</u>: During the rain scene, while everyone is wearing newspapers on their heads, some people shoot water pistols or other kinds of spray guns to simulate rain.

<u>Hot Dogs</u>: When *Brad, Janet* and *Dr. Scott* sing "You're a hot dog" to *Frank-N-Furter*, my friend Marc Shaiman suggested we get hot dogs and throw them. We were the first. Hot dogs, however, never became popular because of their cost. Also, the theater management did not encourage it — meat attracted insects and rats and things, they said, and left stains on the screen. There were the same problems with using prunes, at one time thrown about at their mention in the first song.

The use of lines and props spread rapidly from theater to theater across the country. Hearsay, newspaper and magazine articles, and the fact that New York City <u>ROCKY</u> fans visited theaters playing the show in other parts of the U.S. are the reasons for this phenomenon. The fan club often receives letters from people who have moved from New York, which describe how they use Waverly lines and routines in their home theaters.

John Mandracchia, producer of the first two New York <u>ROCKY HORROR</u> conventions, tells that when visiting Florida on vacation, he brought props to the local theater where the film was playing. The management became quite upset at his throwing rice and cards during the show — they had seen nothing like it before. However, when John returned a year later, the same management thanked him for starting it all.

Costumes and Make-up

In spring of 1977, a young woman named Dori Hartley came to the Waverly to see the <u>RHPS</u> for the first time. No one could guess at the profound effect she was to have on the development of the cult. That night she came with her friend Robin Lipner, who had seen the film a few months before. Dori's reaction to the entire experience, the film itself and the audience antics, coupled with an intense fascination with and attraction to *Frank-N-Furter* (*Frank*), kept her awake most of that night. The next night, although she could not break a previous date in order to see the film, she did ride past the Waverly on her bicycle. It was at 2 a.m., when the crowds were leaving the theater after the show was over. Unable to forget the movie, she went home and sketched portraits of *Frank* from memory. The next Friday she saw the film again. After that, she did not miss a showing of <u>ROCKY</u> until the end of its run at the Waverly six months later.

At first, Dori was threatened by the crowd of regulars, because they were so much a part of the show that so fascinated her. She felt like an outsider. This did not last long. She met Lori Davis, who introduced her to the others in the first row balcony. Lori had seen the show many times and this impressed Dori. She was soon accepted into the "pew" and she and Robin became regulars. She still looked up to the others because they had been in at the beginning of it all, and she was especially impressed by Bill O'Brien, who had played *Frank* in the original floor show.

EARLY FAVORITE AUDIENCE RESPONSES

Magenta: Master, dinner is prepared!
Audience: And we helped!!

☆ ☆

Audience: Is it true that you're constipated?
Criminologist: It's true . . .

☆ ☆

Audience: Do you speak French?
Frank: Enchanté.

☆ ☆

Audience: And Betsy Ross used to sit home and sew and sew . . .
Criminologist: And so . . .

☆ ☆

Audience: F!
Frank: You see?
Audience: K!

The more Dori saw the film, the more her obsession with *Frank* grew. First she dyed her blond hair black, then she had a permanent so she could have the exact hairdo that *Frank* has in the film. At her thirteenth viewing, she appeared wearing make-up identical to *Frank's* and a cape like his that she made herself. Outside, the crowd waiting in line applauded her. She was encouraged by the response, and worked constantly to improve her costume and make-up. It was Dori who re-introduced special clothing for the film and it was here to stay.

When Robin decided to dress up also, Dori suggested that she go as *Magenta*, and she helped with her make-up and with the choosing of a plain black dress. It was about this time that fourteen-year old Maria Medina started coming to the Waverly. She also dressed as *Magenta*, and her maid's costume was complete. In make-up, Maria's resemblance to Patricia

Lori Davis, Dori Hartley and Robin Lipner on the first night Dori wore make-up.

Photo: George Davis

Quinn's *Magenta* in the film was uncanny. Seeing this, Robin finished work on her own costume and wore it. This was the way that the first and most heated of the rivalries between fans wearing the same costume began.

As her act became more polished, Dori began receiving attention and she was approached by Bill O'Brien with the idea of reorganizing the pre-movie floor show. Dori was very excited at this, although disappointed when she realized Bill wanted her to play *Columbia*. Obediently, however, she went home and started to work on the new costume. After all, she still looked up to Bill as the original floor show cast *Frank-N-Furter*.

Bill never got anywhere with his plan, leaving Dori with a half-finished, sequinned *Columbia* outfit. But nothing could dampen her enthusiasm, and it was spreading to the others. When Laura Stein showed interest in dressing up, Dori gave her the

Columbia outfit and helped her with make-up. She herself continued to dress as *Frank-N-Furter*, and suggested to Thom Riley, another regular, that he come as *Riff Raff*; she helped him with costume and make-up, too. In true *Frank-N-Furter* fashion, Dori had built around herself a court of characters.

Forming of Friendships

At first, I did not know anyone other than Marc, who was a habitué of the RHPS. So I started going to the Waverly early each week to meet other fans. Alan Riis became my first friend and he began saving me the fifth row aisle seat. It became my permanent spot. Through Alan, I met Laura Stein (*Columbia*) and Eric Kleiman — one of the first Transylvanians complete with lightning bolt make-up. (Later Eric became the fan club's *Riff Raff*.)

While waiting in line one night, I shouted out a remark to one of my new friends. A young girl came running up to me and said: "It's you. . .you're the one with the voice! I love your voice!" Liz Frank had recognized it from the many lines that I shouted each week. Liz introduced me to her brother Josh and his friend Jude Goldin, and through them I met another regular, Larry Forer, a 30-year old teacher from New Jersey. This began a chain reaction of friendships, which formed the core of the fan club. Now I sat in a block; Larry was behind me, Jude in front. Putting together our lines, bits and props, we formed the "orchestra" people, and began to challenge seriously the dominance of the first row balcony.

We all lived for Friday and Saturday nights. We met at 8 p.m. to make sure that we would be first in line and so get our regular seats. The atmosphere outside the theater was as electric as it was inside. We sang songs, we Time Warped (Once we stopped traffic on Sixth Avenue while we were dancing.), we traded questions, and we waited for the arrival of Dori. All of us shared this devotion to the film as we gathered outside in eager anticipation of midnight.

An early predecessor of the TRANSYLVANIAN, or the fan club newsletter, was distributed by Laura Stein. The TRANSYLVANIAN biweekly or "Mell Tells" (since she played *Columbia*, she called herself "Mell" instead of "Nell") was a two-sided typed sheet that gave information of new audience lines that had been recently created or discontinued and other special events. There was an ongoing debate that the audience line, "she went apeshit," should be discontinued because it came at a special moment, a close-up of *Frank-N-Furter's* face. The balcony group thought it was offensive to yell such a word at that time.

About this time, a quiz began to circulate among those of us who waited in line. Dori, Robin and other regulars began trading ROCKY trivia among themselves and realized just how much information they had in their possession. They came up with the idea of a trivia quiz. Dori and Robin put it together and passed out copies with the heading: "Compliments of Dori and Robin." For the next year and one-half, that quiz was

Sal, Larry Forer (back row), Jude Goldin, Maria Medina and Thom Riley (front row) make up some of the "orchestra people" at The Waverly.

Photo: Roy Morsch

copied and recopied from one side of the country to the other. And through it, Dori and Robin became famous.

I had not actually met either of them. When they handed me a copy of the quiz, I introduced myself as the "voice" from the orchestra who had thrown hot dogs. Their reception was not warm, and they lectured me on the problems that my action had caused. Robin even threatened me, as she jokingly described and acted out a switchblade being snapped open and thrust into someone's belly. At that moment I could not know, and would not have believed, that a long and deep friendship was beginning with these two.

I continued to do my "thing" in the orchestra, although I did stop throwing hot dogs — because of rising meat costs, not Robin's threat. In the beginning I looked at them both as terrible snobs, but I soon saw that this was just their way of protecting the film that they thought was so special. When finally they accepted me as a creative force rather than a destructive one, we became friends. Out of this relationship sprang the famous "balcony-orchestra" wars — with the groups trading lines back and forth throughout the film. For example, when Rocky is eating the meat during the dinner scene, the usual line was "Give it to Mikey, he'll eat anything!" From my seat in the orchestra, I changed it to, "Give it to the balcony, they'll eat anything!" The balcony retorted, "You should know, Sal!"

The two groups tried for weeks to outdo each other, but when it got really out of hand, we called a truce. One night, an anonymous voice in the rear of the balcony yelled a line of derision to the orchestra. Immediately the first row balcony people yelled down in their own defense, "It wasn't us!"

It wasn't long before the theater management received warnings from the fire department about the use of open flames during the candle lighting ceremony. It was a fire hazard, obviously, and even more so since many of the candle bearers wore newspapers on their heads. How could the enthusiasm of the participants be subdued? For a few weeks, ushers and security guards marched up and down the aisles warning people to put out their candles. Mostly, the warnings were ignored.

Then the manager, Denise Borden, came to me, begging me to do something to convince the others that the matter was serious. The fire department had threatened to close the show if the practice of lighting candles did not stop. Denise told me she thought the audience would listen to me because I was one of them.

I thought about it, and that night, when everybody was sitting in their seats, I called for their attention, saying I wished to make an announcement. In as serious a voice as I could muster, I appealed to everyone's good sense, and to their concern that the show go on at the Waverly. I ended with the C-U-R-R-Y cheer, now part of the ritual. Not a candle was lit that night, and from that time on, candles were banned in

---

NOT ALL AUDIENCE LINES ARE RESPONSES TO DIALOGUE. THE AUDIENCE ALSO SHOUTS DIRECTIONS TO THE ACTORS ON THE SCREEN:

Audience: Kick it!
- *Brad* kicks the tire.

☆ ☆

Audience: Drop it!
- *Riff Raff* drops the bottle.

☆ ☆

Audience: Come a little bit closer.
- *Criminologist* leans forward.

☆ ☆

Audience: Show us your ear, *Frank.*
- *Dr. Frank-N-Furter* pulls back his hair and reveals his ear.

many theaters everywhere. The practice of making general announcements before the film started then. I myself made many of them — about birthdays, celebrations, and transylversaries.[1] I seemed to be the one who made the announcements, for the most part and I became known as spokesman for the ROCKY HORROR cult in New York. Once we started the fan club and I became President of it, this became a natural role for me.

The All-New Floor Show

Everyone wanted to be part of the creative action. Every week some new idea was tried out and developed, but we were yet to create the audience participation that was going to make our group famous.

The original pre-movie floor show had disbanded. But now, with the popularity of the film gaining constantly, rumors began to circulate that the floor show was going to be revived. Many regulars started to come dressed as characters from the film, following the example of Dori and her friends. We had a complete cast now, so why not organize a floor show ourselves? We spontaneously came up with what seemed like a logical extension to what had gone before: the holding of a live floor show during the movie.

Anyone who has seen the RHPS a few times knows how to do the "Time Warp." "It's just a jump to the left, then a step to the right..." I'm sure that at every theater where ROCKY is showing, people have stood up at their seats or gone into the aisles to dance. At the Waverly, the number of Time Warpers kept increasing. One night a few of us really let loose. When *Riff Raff* and *Magenta* opened the doors to the ballroom, we ran up in front of the screen and performed the dance in full view of the audience. Of course, during the solo verses, we bent down out of sight. Once, though, on the spur of the moment, I stood up and mimicked *Columbia's* tap dance in sync with the film. The applause afterward was encouraging; clearly the audience was ready for a new variety of participation. The Time Warp made a good starting point, because everyone could join in with the dancing.

Time Warp Instructions
1. (It's just a) Jump to the left, with hands up.
2. A step to the right (Time Warper Annette Funicello suggests a very wide step.)
3. (With your hands on your hips)[2]
   You bring your knees in tight.
4. (Then) The pelvic thrust (If repeated five times, it nearly drives you insa-a-ane.)

---

1. transylversary /tran/syl/ver/sar/y (n) — the anniversary of a special number of viewings of the RHPS, i.e. 50, 100, 200 times.

2. Those with limb disabilities may find it necessary to alter or delete this action, but no excuses for alterations to steps four and five.

DEPENDING ON THE POSITION OR HEIGHT OF THE SCREEN AT A THEATER — SOME AUDIENCE MEMBERS HAVE DEVELOPED PHYSICAL ROUTINES WITH THE SCREEN.

When the church custodian (played by Richard O'Brien) throws the pitchfork from the steps — someone below the screen falls down as if hit.

☆ ☆

When *Janet* starts to sing "Toucha-Toucha-Touch Me" in her bra and slip, a pair of hands from the audience will "Toucha-Toucha-Touch" her.

☆ ☆

At the end when *Brad, Janet* and *Dr. Scott* are left behind on the ground the screen begins to spin ably assisted by a group from the audience. When the spinning turns into a globe — the criminologist stops the spinning and the audience assistants fall to the ground.

5. Hipswivel (If not driven insa-a-ane by step four.)
6. Let's do the Time Warp again!!

Out of this came the individual members of the audience taking on specific characterizations and acting out scenes simultaneously with their screen counterparts. Dori's wardrobe continued growing, until everything *Frank* wore was included. One night, during "Sword of Damocles," when she was wearing the green surgical robe, she persuaded a blond, *Rocky*-type regular named John to strip to his underwear. Right on cue, as *Frank* chased *Rocky* on the screen, Dori began chasing John around the theater. Audience participation finally had reached the level of true theatrics.

As for myself, I became more and more fascinated with the *Janet* character. (<u>Fascinated</u>, <u>not obsessed</u> — for I was not about to dye my hair blond!) I marvelled at Susan Sarandon's performance and I participated in many of her scenes. When Betty Monroe threw the bouquet, I jumped in my seat and pretended to catch it at the same time as *Janet* did. One night a girl named Ellen brought me a bouquet to catch — and so I had my first *Janet* prop. I also played another scene, the one when *Janet* shows off her ring saying, "It's nicer than Betty Monroe had." Betty Rice and Alba Cordasco, two school-teacher friends of Larry, brought an oversized rhinestone ring

Dori Hartley in Frank's green surgical gown.

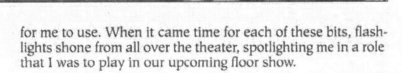

Sal shows off rhinestone ring which is "nicer than Betty Monroe had."

for me to use. When it came time for each of these bits, flashlights shone from all over the theater, spotlighting me in a role that I was to play in our upcoming floor show.

As the weeks went on, members began to establish themselves in specific character roles. The first *Janet* and *Brad* were Donna Bruggerman and Alba Cordasco. Donna was an innocent-seeming blond from Staten Island who, once inside the theater, stripped to a bra and slip and played *Janet's* scenes inside the castle. Alba was dressed, like *Brad*, in a tuxedo, plaid tie and cummerbund. It became standard for Alba and me to get up in our seats and kiss at the end of the line, "Dammit *Janet*." I had now added a wedding hat to my wardrobe.

Marc Shaiman brought Mickey Mouse ears and a hair dryer, and for a while, during "Toucha-Toucha-Touch Me," he and I mimicked *Columbia* and *Magenta* from our seats. One night, we went up to the small stage below the level of the screen itself and did the number before the whole house. We were all getting bolder and bolder in what we wanted to do. The climax came when Dori, in her completed "Sweet Transvestite" outfit, performed the entire number in front of the screen and up and down the aisles.

After this, anything went. Thom Riley performed as *Riff Raff* during "There's a Light." At other times, he or Paul Gheradi (our other *Riff*) did the Time Warp with Robin or Maria, our dueling *Magentas*. There were bannisters at the sides of the steps down to the orchestra at the Waverly. One night Robin slid down the bannister on the left, throwing her feather duster

Alba Cordasco and Donna Bruggerman, The Waverly's first Brad and Janet.

Mike Morra (Eddie), Robin Lipner and Dori at The Waverly.

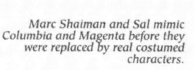

Marc Shaiman and Sal mimic Columbia and Magenta before they were replaced by real costumed characters.

Thom Riley (Riff) and Maria Medina (Magenta) outside The Waverly.

Donna and Sal — Will the real Janet please stand up?

Sal and his Dr. Scott Sing-A-Long book.

to *Riff Raff*, at the same time as *Magenta* made a similarly magnificent entrance on screen. Laura Stein (*Columbia*) and Mike Morra (*Janet*) danced in the aisles during "Hot Patootie." It became natural that Maria, in her *Magenta* negligee, and Laura, in her pajamas, replaced Marc and me during "Toucha." Donna, still in bra and slip, wanted to do the "Toucha" number, but she needed a *Rocky*. There was no one resembling Rocky around, so I volunteered, turning the number into a hilarious routine embellished by high camp. From that day on, we never performed that particular number seriously — or later either, when I was playing *Janet*.

I created one bit that I was particularly proud of because I was not mimicking something from the film. This was the use of the audience cue cards during "*Eddie's* Teddy." The audience had always echoed each line of the song when it was sung by *Dr. Scott*. Now I devised a giant songbook containing all the responses, with a few "sha-bop-sha-bop-bops" thrown in, and writing *Dr. Scott's* lines with a German accent.

Alan Riis had a marvelous sense of humor. He had a ventriloquist's dummy that he named "Larabee." Alan dressed this dummy as *Rocky*, and Larabee performed at a number of ROCKY theaters. I had the privilege (?) to perform "Toucha" with Larabee a few times when the dummy wasn't performing with Joy, Alan's favorite *Janet*.

It had by now been established that Dori and I were the driving forces of the floor show, whose cult following was growing rapidly. Dori's glamorous and dramatic portrayal of *Dr. Frank-N-Furter* combined well with my comic interpretations. What might have been only a passing fad was turning into an important cultural statement.

As 1977 was ending, we were on top of the world and having the time of our lives. In our wildest imaginations, though, we never dreamed of the dramatic future lying ahead for the cult of RHPS audience participation. Already the media — newspapers, magazines, you name it — had begun to pick up on what was going on at the Waverly.

Rocky Horror

The Rocky Horror Groupies

he Waverly is an ordinary movie house ex-
pt every Friday and Saturday at midnight
hen the "Rocky Horror Picture Show" goes
n. Then, dressed like the movie's characters,
e howling cult takes over

JOHNNY GREENE

he cult stands poised and preened and impa-
nt on the sidewalk at the Waverly Theater
the Village, ready to storm inside for a
turday night showing of the "Rocky Horror
cture Show." For them, "Rocky Horror" has
come a way of life. Some have seen it more
an a hundred times but there are a few here
night who have never seen it before. Cult
embers call them "virgins." One kid tells me
's been here longer than three hours, stand-
continued on page 18

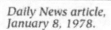

*Daily News article,
January 8, 1978.*

he happenings at the Waverly Theater naturally generated much excitement, word of mouth and publicity. The ROCKY HORROR PICTURE SHOW and our
floor show were the hottest tickets in town. There were major
newspaper articles written about us. The New York Daily
News did a big Sunday Magazine feature on us, complete with
full color studio photos of Dori Hartley and the other regulars
in costume.

Previous to the Daily News article, the first writer to let people
in on all of this was Arthur Bell in his weekly column in the
Village Voice. After detailing all the fun of the evening's events,
he predicted that the publicity would bring curiosity seekers
and troublemakers who would spoil the fun.

Mr. Bell was absolutely right. This publicity did bring a lot of
curiosity seekers to stare at the "freaks" in costume. Also,

'Rocky' horrors

Uniondale, L.I.: This is to inform you of our
dissatisfaction with Johnny Greene's "The
Rocky Horror Picture Show." We, loyal fol-
lowers of the "Horror Show" and Uniondale's
Mini Cinema, have always taken pride in
what we're sure Mr. Greene would've refer-
red to as our "cult," had he investigated other
movie houses in the metropolitan area. For
Mr. Greene to have discussed the movie as
though it only thrived at the Waverly is gross-
ly inaccurate. Many of us have seen "Rocky
Horror" over 50 times and our overall inven-
tiveness has been the equal of the Waverly's
congregation, and in the invention of new
lines and the use of props, far superior.
LIHSF
(LI Horror Show Fans—40 names)

*Letter to Daily News reflecting
the jealousy of the publicity received by The Waverly.*

there were many people who stood in long lines trying to get into an already sold-out house. Sixth Avenue became a traffic hazard and the local Block Association and businesses began to petition against the Waverly and the film, complaining about the crowds and the noise.

Even worse than that was the youth gang from the Little Italy section a few blocks away. They came to make trouble for the "faggots and weirdos," in fishnets and makeup. This was a violent, racist gang who did not want us near their neighborhood or "turf." Things started getting worse around Christmas of 1977 and there were some horrible incidents in January of 1978. To this day, I think the gang was actually encouraged by some of the merchants to cause trouble in order to get the film closed down.

On Saturday in late January, the early show at the Waverly was Bob Dylan's "Reynaldo and Clara," a four-hour plus film which began at eight o'clock, meaning ROCKY wouldn't be coming on until after midnight, probably 12:30 or 12:45. This meant more time in line for those of us waiting out in the street in the freezing January air. The gang members were also out on the street, causing trouble. Some of them even had baseball bats. When the entrance to the Waverly finally opened, people rushed the doors. It was a mob scene and someone got clobbered with a baseball bat. Those of us who were toward the front got in first and were happy to escape without injury, but we were scared — for ourselves, for those outside and for our weekly party.

Did you know — *that at the end of the seven-year run of the ROCKY HORROR play in London, Janet was played by Tracy Ullman?*

At first, we were all very timid about doing our thing, but as the night progressed, we were back to our usual spirited fun. As an aftermath of the violence, however, the Waverly decided to close down the film, and that was our last night there.

And so we were homeless, but ROCKY HORROR fever was catching on, and midnight showings, complete with floor shows, were cropping up everywhere all over the country. In a few weeks, the Waverly fan group received an offer from the management of the Arion Theater in Middle Village, Queens, New York. (Queens is a borough adjacent to Manhattan.) They wanted us to perform our show twice a week at their theater. They would provide round-trip bus transportation for our cast and free admission. They also provided transportation for any of the other Waverly regulars or people who wanted to come and buy a ticket at their theater.

Violence followed us again. The buses picked us up in front of the Waverly, so naturally, we would receive a royal send-off from our "good" friends, the youth gang, and receive an even bigger welcome from a gang of kids from Queens. Ice balls and shovels replaced the baseball bats in February. After a few weeks, ROCKY HORROR closed at the Arion and we were moved to another theater in Queens. The Center Theater was owned by the same people, but it was located in a much better neighborhood.

After a slow start, we settled in at the Center. A loyal following developed and the theater sold out regularly. Our floor show and the fan club that we had formed while at the Waverly flourished. We were content.

Then the Walter Reade Organization opened ROCKY at another of their theaters in midtown Manhattan, the Festival. It became the new home of the Waverly print of the movie. At first, it did not do well, and we chose to stay in Queens where we were well-treated and given transportation. Gradually, a floor show developed at the Festival and it began to sell out; many of our regulars wanted to go back home to Manhattan. A lot of in-fighting developed and our group began to split up over this. Should we invade the Festival or stay faithful to those people in Queens, even though it meant traveling every time? What should we do? Again, I felt like it was all falling apart.

In late June, Larry and Jude were walking down 8th Street in the Village and there was a sign in the newly-reopened Eighth Street Playhouse: "Opening soon - The ROCKY HORROR PICTURE SHOW." They immediately went in to speak to the owners, Steve Hirsch and Mark Hoffehr, and told them who we were. Knowing all about us from the Waverly, they welcomed our group with open arms. With regrets to the owners in Queens who had helped keep our floor show alive those six months, we went home to the Village, where we belonged.

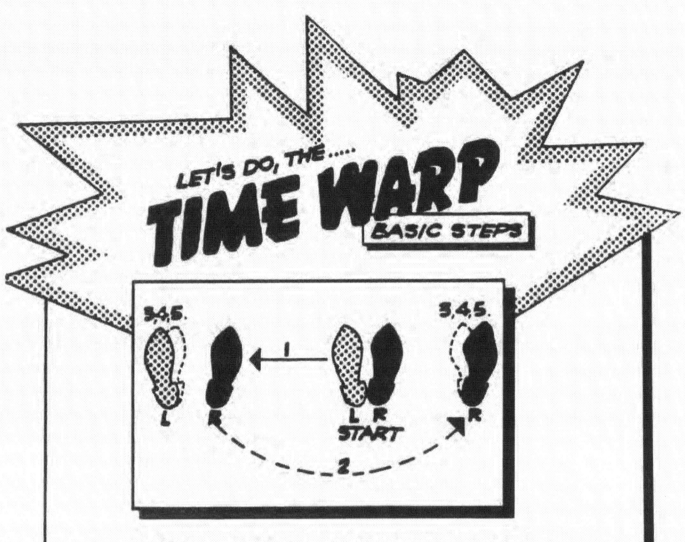

1 (IT'S JUST A) **JUMP TO THE LEFT**, WITH HANDS **UP!**
2 A **STEP TO THE RIGHT** (TIME-WARPER **ANNETTE FUNICELLO**
                            SUGGESTS A VERY **WIDE** STEP.)
3* (WITH YOUR HANDS ON YOUR **HIPS**)
   YOU BRING YOUR KNEES IN TIGHT.
4 (THEN) **THE PELVIC THRUST** (IF REPEATED **FIVE** TIMES, IT
                            NEARLY DRIVES YOU INSA-A-ANE)
5 **HIPSWIVEL** (IF NOT DRIVEN INSA-A-ANE BY STEP FOUR)
6 **LET'S DO THE TIME WARP AGAIN!!**
* THOSE WITH **LIMB DISABILITIES** MAY FIND IT NECESSARY
   TO **ALTER** OR **DELETE** THIS ACTION, BUT **NO EXCUSES**
   FOR ALTERATIONS TO STEPS FOUR AND FIVE.

17

Brian Thomson

AS FEATURED IN *'THE ROCKY HORROR SHOW'*

Various articles on Playhouse
- *Rolling Stone*
- *New York Times*
- *After Dark*
- *The Villager*

After six months of wandering around the boroughs as a "nomad" floor show, we were finally returning home to the Village. The Eighth Street Playhouse, where we were going to perform, is located about four blocks away from the Waverly in Greenwich village. At first we were a little worried about a repeat of the earlier problems, but our fears were quickly put aside. The Playhouse was on a cross street and not a main avenue, so we did not cause traffic problems. Also, we were beyond the "turf" of that local gang, who had tried to terrorize us when we were at the Waverly.

The owners of the Eighth Street Playhouse further insured our safety by having a well-trained security staff. From that first night, July 17, 1978, we were sold out and for the next eleven years we played to mostly sold out houses. In fact, during the early years there, ticket demand was so high that we had to watch out for scalpers selling the $3.50 tickets (the price in the late 70's) for $10 and $15. We had the full cooperation of the two owners who were aware that our performing group was part of the attraction. Our performers were rewarded with free tickets and early access to the theater in order to dress and makeup. (This is a common practice around the country by theater owners smart enough to realize the benefits of a cast/performing group.)

Dori performs in the aisles to an attentive audience.

Photo: Fredda Tone

Ad for 8th Street Playhouse with billing for Sal and the cast.

Debbie Schott performs in front of painted backdrop of RKO Tower.

3rd Anniversary
cake by Christine
MacNamee

Photo: Fredda Tone

The first night at Eighth Street was amazing. We returned to a
sold-out house. We did a preshow of the Time Warp, and then
I came on to do the night's announcements which, since the
Waverly, had developed into part of our ritual. The first words
out of my mouth were, "We're back in the Village!" The whole
audience stood and cheered. We had returned to a dream sit-
uation without all the hassles and problems.

There was a resurgence of publicity with articles in After Dark
magazine, New York magazine, the Village Voice, and spots
on local television.

The only problem of our return was that we no longer had a
full cast. Some people had dropped out during our exile in
Queens. Dori was out of town seeing Tim Curry in concert at
the Roxy in L.A. My younger sister Lillias and her friends had
formed a cast that now performed in some theaters in New Jersey. I had brought Lillias to the Waverly when she was 12
years old, with my mother's disapproval. In fact, she used to
say to me, "Why are you wasting your time? What will you get
out of this?" (Who would have realized?) My sister fell in love
with the movie and Tim Curry and the character of Magenta
(more competition for Robin?).

Lillias and her New Jersey cast were persuaded to come back
to New York and join us on Eighth Street. This gave us a very
complete cast with backups in most parts. As the weeks and
months went on, we added more things to our preshow. Besides the "Time Warp," "Sweet Transvestite" became a regular
feature and my preshow announcements got longer.

These announcements consisted of reading and commenting
on notes that were given to me by people in the audience to
welcome or tease their "virgin" friends, for birthday celebra-

tions, to announce someone's transylversary (numbers in the 100's were becoming very common), and lots of private jokes which soon became public jokes. One of the reasons why the announcements became longer was, as more people came, more people wanted me to read notes and embarrass their friends.

Eventually, our preshow expanded from ten minutes to forty minutes, and we began to get hassled by Steve, one of the owners. The other owner, Mark, was "laid back" and didn't bother us, but Steve began to get difficult. After a few years, Mark and Steve decided to break up their partnership. One was going to sell out to the other. We were hoping that Mark would buy out Steve, but as luck would have it, Steve became sole owner of Eighth Street.

Dori poses with Kim Canonico, 10 year old Frank-N-Furter, winner of Halloween Costume Contest 1978.

Kim Canonico performs with an all-children cast at 8th Street Playhouse.

What followed was a five to six year stormy relationship between Steve and myself and the cast. Steve began to resent the fact that my name, not his, became attached to the Eighth Street Playhouse. I started to get phone calls from all over the world from fans or journalists trying to reach me. Steve would hang up on them saying, "Sal Piro does not work here." He would go on tirades and start problems with the cast or give us time limits for our preshow. But his new rules and edicts didn't last long because the bottom line was that the Playhouse was selling out every weekend and making money. ROCKY HOR-ROR was paying his rent and he needed us, so he could only go so far. In the end, we would usually win out.

The Playhouse was our home, our playground, our church, our regular meeting place twice a week. Over the years, we did some extraordinary things. We had many special events. Our guest visitors, included: Susan Sarandon, Gene Simmons of Kiss, Cliff Robertson, Dina Merrill, Tommy Shaw of Styx, and local television personalities. There was always electricity in the air, making each night a special event. We had joke door prizes, gags and special features. One night, we recreated "We are the World," with everyone dressed as rock stars and ROCKY HORROR characters. There was a special raffle that night for USA for Africa.

Another time, we had a murder mystery night, that we called "Who killed Moishe?" (Our nickname for Seth, our *criminologist*). Years later this was repeated as "Who will kill Kawkeye?" (Our rather loud *Eddie*).

The night that stands out in the minds of many Eighth Street regulars was the night of "Michelle and Moishe's wedding." Michelle Rehfeld and Seth (Moishe) Bogdanove were two members of the floor show. I approached them in January for a grand practical joke that I was planning for April Fool's week. No one else was in on this joke. In late January, Moishe asked Michelle on a date. Michelle began to tell friends of her blossoming romance with Moishe. Then it was revealed that Michelle was pregnant and Moishe couldn't face up to it. Meanwhile, nothing really was going on, for Michelle and Moishe weren't even good friends. After everyone found out Michelle was "pregnant," she acted very depressed, until one March night at ROCKY, Moishe proposed to Michelle in front of the entire audience. She accepted and the two received a standing ovation. They were to be married in April, on stage at the Eighth Street Playhouse. It was to be the "night of nights" at the theater.

Since Michelle and Moishe were Jewish, I hired someone to play a rabbi. The wedding was announced on a local radio station, and tickets to ROCKY HORROR sold out early in the day. Michelle arrived in a gorgeous wedding gown. As she came down the aisle, with Brendan Conboy as *Frank* to give her away, my friend, professional singer Gary Reed sang, "You Light Up My Life," adding a tacky yet sentimental touch.

The rabbi began the ceremony. Then he said those predictable words, "If there is anyone here who knows why these two

Susan Sarandon visits the Playhouse.

Brendon Conboy (Frank) brings Bride-To-Be Michelle down the aisle.

Moishe and Michelle prepare to exchange vows??

should not be married, let them speak now or forever hold their peace." At this point, another person we had recruited, all shabbily dressed, came running down the aisle yelling "Michelle, wait! You can't marry him! You know the baby's mine!" Everyone was aghast! I approached the center of the stage, grabbed the microphone, and announced "Ladies and gentlemen, there is no baby, there is no wedding." Then Michelle, Moishe and I shouted in unison, "April Fools!" The lights went out and the movie began. People were screaming, they couldn't believe it. Some were laughing, some were crying, some were just plain mad at being duped. To this day, I have never been able to top this joke.

In July of 1986, Steve Hirsch died and we arrived at the theater and found it was closed. We were very confused and afraid we would lose our home. But the theater was only closed a few weeks. The B.S. Moss Company bought the theater from the estate and it reopened with most of the old staff. Steve's former assistant managers now were in charge of the place. Since they were only on salary and had no vested interest in the theater, they were not pleased with the length of our show. They were young and wanted to get out of work with enough time to go to the local clubs. One of the managers began to come down hard on me and the cast, limiting our show, and in some cases, announcing in the middle of my act that I had 5 minutes. Once he even started the movie while I was still talking.

Rather than argue with someone fifteen years my junior who was on a power trip, I made an appointment with one of the general managers of the Moss Company. I showed him all my clippings, books and other proof that we had helped bring great fame to the playhouse and great box office besides. I told him of all the grief I had gone through with Steve and his ego and what we were now going through. I said that I didn't want any money (music to a businessman's ears), just some respect from the staff and the time to do what we were used to doing. That very next Friday, it was as if the red carpet had been rolled out and for the next two years we had no problems. Paradise continued at the Eighth Street Playhouse.

Then the owners, B. S. Moss, arranged for United Artists to manage their theater and eventually sold it to them. In September of 1989, we received terrible news, United Artists had sold the Playhouse to City Cinemas and since United Artists had the contract to show ROCKY, we must move. They transferred us to one of their other theaters, the Eastside Cinema, uptown, on 55th Street and 3rd Avenue. It was like starting all over from the beginning. It was very slow at first, but we began building a strong and loyal following again. That is where we are today.

A PERSONAL NOTE

I was very sad to leave the Eighth Street Playhouse. When we had left the Waverly, everything was still very new to us, and the fact that there was a threat of continued violence had left fear in us then. But Eighth Street was a special place, a home for me and the hundreds of castmates who became friends while participating in their mutual admiration for RHPS.

I watched so many people come and go. It was strange watching people leave ROCKY — but they would only leave physically — for the movie and its experience will stay with them forever.

It was very sad when Dori Hartley retired back in 1981-82. Dori had put five solid years into her make-up, costumes, performance, energy, artwork and love for ROCKY. More than any other floor show performer, she left her mark on ROCKY HORROR. I still get letters to this day asking about her and whether she is still performing.

My sister Lillias also retired. She had put almost ten years into ROCKY HORROR, and it is especially sad, looking across the theater and not seeing her in her usual seat.

I must say, however, that one of the reasons that ROCKY HORROR has survived is because there were always more wonderful people to replace those who had come before them.

I am especially grateful to the long-running *Frank-N-Furters* we had at the Playhouse. *Frank-N-Furters* have the most costume changes, most difficult make-up and need the most energy. To those *"Franks"* — Dori, Natalie, Doug, Debbie B., Debbie S., Terry, Carla, Brendon, Julie, Glenn, Perry, Jackie, Barbara, Donny, Delfina, Tracey and Seth — I say, "Thank You!!!"

In 1987, without my knowledge, I was entered into the Guinness Book of World Records. The book listed me as having seen one film (ROCKY HORROR) more than anyone else. The number that they used was 873 times, which was the number of times that I had claimed at the Tenth Anniversary two years before. By the time they book came out, I had already seen the movie over one thousand (1,000) times.

For the next two years, I attended Guinness Conventions and press conferences. I met many strange, interesting and unique people (My favorite was the man who caught grapes in his mouth when they were dropped off of buildings.)

I was eliminated from the 1989 edition of the book, because of their claim that the Fan Club was supported by the studio (20th Century Fox), and since I worked for the studio, the Guinness people said that my record was invalid. The truth was that I had achieved this record before the Studio began giving assistance to the Fan Club. I wasn't being paid to see the movie, twice a week, for over thirteen years. That was my choice.

RIPLEY'S-*BELIEVE IT OR NOT!*

THE WORLD'S # MOVIE FAN-- OF ONE MOVIE! SAL PIRO OF JERSEY CITY, N.J., HAS SEEN THE CULT FILM, "THE ROCKY HORROR PICTURE SHOW," OVER 1,100 TIMES —EQUIVALENT TO VIEWING IT EVERY DAY FOR MORE THAN THREE YEARS

© 1982 King Features Syndicate Inc. World rights reserved

From the Guinness Book of World Records

SINGLE-MOVIE VIEWING RECORD

Sal Piro of New York City has seen "The Rocky Horror Picture Show" 873 times during its 11-year run in the city.

From the GUINNESS BOOK OF WORLD RECORDS 1987, published by permission of Sterling Publishing Co., Inc., New York. © 1986 by Guinness Superlatives Ltd.

My one thousandth performance at <u>ROCKY HORROR</u> was celebrated in April of 1987. The special guest of the evening was Richard O'Brien, who sang "Time Warp" live with my sister Lillias and Maria Parisi. This was another of the many great highlights of my <u>ROCKY</u> experience.

Perry and Jack close in on Eastside Cinema Riff Raff (Mad Man Mike).

Photo: Teddy Sexton

Justin Sheps (Magenta) does his Vanna White act to welcome Richard O'Brien to 8th Street.

Richard O'Brien appears at Sal's 1000th performance.

This is Sal's favorite cast photo.

Photo: Lou Gonzalez

Richard O'Brien, Lillias Piro and Maria Parisi perform "Time Warp" live at Sal's 1000th performance.

Evolution of fan club
membership cards.
1. 1977
2. 1980
3. 1985

While we were at the Waverly, we wanted to celebrate our love for ROCKY HORROR in a special way. We thought a ROCKY HORROR convention would be a good idea. Larry Forer thought that since we didn't have any money to front the convention we should form a fan club or fan organization. Through this club, we would raise money for a convention. A group of us met during the week. This group included; Dori, Robin, Larry, Jude, David Hahn and other Waverly regulars.

At that meeting there were nominations for officers. Both Dori and I were nominated to run for President. Just as we were about to vote Dori removed herself from the running because she wasn't interested in heading the organization. I won the position uncontested. That is how I became the President of the newlyformed National ROCKY HORROR Fan Club. Larry Forer was named Vice President and Dori became our Artists-in-Residence. She designed the original membership card and the fan club button that was given as a premium for joining. We offered both a year's membership or a one-half year's membership. Work began on the Transylvanian, the fan club newsletter, with Robin Lipner as our Editor.

THE ROCKY HORROR FAN CLUB
111 morton st. suite 4a nyc 10014

President	Sal Piro
Vice President	Larry Forer
Treasurer	Robert Schmitt
Secretary	Jude V. Goldin
Sargeant-at-Arms	Dori Hartley
Editor	Robin Lipner

EXECUTIVE COMMITTEE

Jane Averbach	Elaine Hall
Ed Boredenka	Eric Kleiman
Janice Bromberg	Sandee Kapolowitz
Sarah Golfleah	Peter Pouridas
Gail Gold	Adam Sargin
David Hahn	Rose Ann Socci

Creatures of the Night,

The following is a report to you about the affairs of YOUR fan club. We all feel very strongly that you, the backbone of this organization, has the right and responsibility to know of the workings and activities of this club.

If you have any questions, comments or just wish to drop a line, please do. We really enjoy hearing from our "Rocky" friends. Also, as a gift of the fan club, please accept this button of Frank N. Furter.

Sincerely,

Rocky Horror Fan Club
Executive Board

The Transylvanian

Original officers and executive
board of the fan club.

Original introduction letter
of fan club. Artwork by Dori.

Evolution of fan club applications, 1977–1985.

The early Transylvanians that were published in 1978 were not typed, but hand printed, thanks to the perseverance and hard work of our Artist-in-Residence, Dori. (Later issues were printed by Peter Pouridas.) These Transylvanians included: fiction, reviews of other theaters, artwork, puzzles, interviews (one with Little Nell), personals, and Transylvanian News Flashes, which were updates on the ROCKY HORROR stars and the cult.

The 4 early Transylvanians, January – July 1978.

As the fan club grew, we became more ambitious with the printing of the newsletter and set our sights on developing it into a real magazine or fanzine. With the help of a young man named Adam Sargis, we were able to publish our first magazine, Transylvanian #1, in the fall of 1978.

First <u>Transylvanian</u> magazine,
Fall of "78".

Second <u>Transylvanian</u> magazine,
February, 1979.

Adam was a free-lance merchandiser and ROCKY HORROR T-shirt salesman. He helped us by getting advertisements and funding for the printing. That first issue was a big success for us. However, we had some differences of opinion with Adam about the purpose of the magazine and the fan club and we parted company. Adam went on to start his own fan club, the International ROCKY HORROR Fan Club.

We printed our second Transylvanian in early 1979, which included wonderful photos of Tim Curry in concert. At this time, Tim Curry was on a national tour promoting his new A & M record album, "Read My Lips." As a nice tribute to all the ROCKY HORROR fans who attended his concerts, Tim ended his show by singing "I'm Going Home."

At this time David Hahn, our *Riff Raff* and board member of the fan club, introduced me to his friend Alex Gorby. Alex was active in fandom and very interested in ROCKY HORROR. He became our business manager and we became friends. We flew out to Los Angeles, at mostly our own expense, to meet with the licensing people at Twentieth Century Fox and to get legal permission to use the lips and logo for our club.

While out there, we made contact with merchandisers and other connections that would help the fan club. Alex then began work on what was our most ambitious project to date, Transylvanian #3, a 36-page ROCKY HORROR fan magazine, complete with a full-color cover. It was beautiful. Alex had made a deal with a big magazine distributor to fund the magazine in exchange for distribution and merchandising rights. We were all so excited about our growth and the realization that at last our fan club convention would come to be.

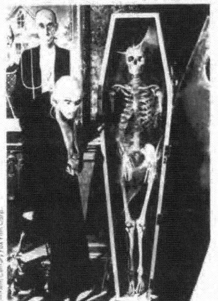

One night, while the cast of the floor show was still at the Waverly, we were approached by a young man named John Mandracchia, who told us of an upcoming convention he was planning at a concert hall in Long Island. He said that a lot of the film's stars would be there. At first, we didn't believe him. Later we found out this enterprising young man and his friend, pharmacist Paul Spiegel, were the co-producers of the first ROCKY HORROR convention. It was to be held on February 20, 1977 at 8 p.m. at the Calderone Concert Hall in Hempstead, Long Island. Even though we were not associated with them, they acknowledged my being president of the newly-formed fan club. So, John asked me to give the welcome and do the cheers.

The place was packed, nearly 2000 people. I worked the crowd into a frenzy with a welcome and cheers. As I walked off, a man on the side of the stage said to me, "Good warmup." It was Richard O'Brien. My mouth opened wide. It was the first of many times that I would meet this wonderful man. I would like to say that of all the people I have met connected to ROCKY, he is the most special person. A witty, creative, sensitive individual with a real love for people and his work, he always finds time to give to any fan. I will always have nothing but the greatest respect and love for him. Thank you, Richard, for this wonderful movie.

The other guests at this convention were: Pat Quinn (*Magenta*), Little Nell (*Columbia*) and Meatloaf (*Eddie*). When Richard, Pat and Nell sang "Time Warp," and when Meatloaf sang "Hot Patootie," the crowd went wild. There was also a costume contest. As a goof, I put on my bra and slip from my bag of props and costumes, threw on a blonde wig and stormed on stage doing *Janet's* "What's happening here?" speech. The celebrity judges thought it was very funny and believe it or not I was one of the ten finalists. I lost to a *Frank-N-Furter* from Long Island with real tattoos.

ATTENTION
ROCKY HORROR FANS!!!
Come To "THE ROCKY HORROR SHOW" Convention
Monday Night — February 20th - 8 P.M.

Presented by
JOHN MANDRACCHIA
&
PAUL SPIEGEL

at the
CALDERONE CONCERT HALL
145 N. Franklin St. • Hempstead, L.I. N.Y.

SEE LIVE IN PERSON!
☆ RICHARD O'BRIEN (Riff Raff)
☆ PATRICIA QUINN (Magenta)
☆ LITTLE NELL (Columbia)

Tickets: $10.00 In Advance
$12.00 Night of Convention if not sold out

Tickets Available Feb. 1st at all Ticketron Outlets.

Also call ROCKY HORROR HOT LINE for additional information
(212) 531-6372
From 9 A.M. - 9 A.M. and 6 P.M. - 2 A.M.
AT OTHER TIMES THE ROCKY HORROR TAPE WILL BE HEARD
Calderone Theater: (516) 481-4600

Dori Hartley and Waverly regulars pose for photos at Calderone Convention.

Ticket for Second Convention.

Spiegel and Mandracchia followed their big success with another convention on October 8, 1978, at the same place. The guests for this one were Pat Quinn, Jonathan Adams (Dr. Scott), and at the last moment Tim Curry and Susan Sarandon were booked to make an appearance. The crowd reaction was even wilder than the one before. When Tim Curry came on stage, the screams were deafening. Susan Sarandon actually looked very startled by the crowd. This time, John asked me to run the costume contest, so my Janet routine was not eligible. It was a thrill to be on the same stage as the stars.

When Jonathan Adams was booked for the convention, he expressed interest to John in wanting to do his cabaret act somewhere. John asked me to help because I had a cabaret comedy act that I performed occasionally. So I was able to get Jonathan Adams booked at the Duplex in the Village and I was his opening act.

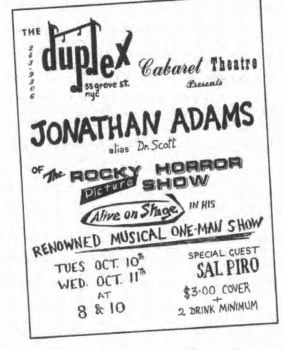

Jonathan Adams poses with Sal after Duplex show.

Jonathan's act was brilliant and funny. He played many characters and sang some satirical songs that were witty and intelligent. I think his English sense of humor went over the heads of some of the younger fans. The fact that Tim Curry was playing the same night eight blocks away at the Bottom Line didn't help attendance. Jonathan, however, attracted some loyal fans.

Thanks to these two successful conventions produced by John and Paul, our group and the fan club became more established in the eyes of the stars and the fans.

THE FAN CLUB CONVENTION FAILURE

After the success of the two Long Island ROCKY HORROR conventions, the fan club still wanted to have their own convention. After all, the original reason for starting the fan club was to have a convention.

Two members of our group, Alex Gorby and David Hahn, decided they wanted to produce the convention in conjunction with the fan club. At least, I thought they were both a little young, but Alex, at 19, had previous experience working in fandom with Star Trek conventions. Also, he had his own skateboard business when he was fourteen. David was sixteen, but had years of experience with merchandising and was much more mature than his age. They formed their own company YES (Youth Entrepreneurial Services) and began to plan the "convention to beat all conventions." They made a down payment and booked the Palladium (one of the biggest concert halls in Manhattan) for Saturday, October 28, 1979. They made a deal with a local promoter to co-sponsor a ROCKY HORROR Halloween Party three nights later at Roseland Ballroom.

The promoter gave YES money to bring in the stars of the film from England in return for their appearance at Roseland. They booked Richard O'Brien, Pat Quinn, Jonathan Adams, Little Nell, set designer Brian Thomson and costume designer Sue Blane.

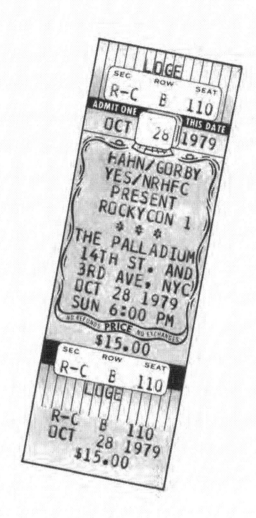

Posters, buttons and T-shirts were printed, advertisements appeared in the paper, plane tickets were booked, and hotel rooms were reserved. Everything seemed to be going extremely well. What I didn't know was that these young producers had no reserve-cash fund. They were paying for everything, as they received the money from advance ticket sales.

As the great day approached, ticket sales were sluggish and bills were growing. Many people were probably waiting until the last minute to buy their tickets or pay at the door. Then the day arrived. The final payment for the Palladium was due, the stars were on their way from England, and there was no money left. The Palladium would not allow us in without that money. What to do? Cancel??

At the last minute, it seemed like our only alternative was to cancel, but there were fans arriving from all over the Northeast and even places as far away as Chicago and California. All the stars were at that minute over the Atlantic Ocean. As a final desperation move, one of the producers found a downtown club called Heat which would take us in. People were diverted from the Palladium and given directions to Heat. Anyone with advance tickets was honored at the door, but anyone who paid at the door, that money went right to the club for the rental. Also, the club kept all the money from the food and drinks.

The show that night was electrifying. Richard, Pat, Nell, Jonathan and Dori as *Frank* gave wonderful performances. At the end of the show, Richard took out a guitar, sat on stage, and sang for a half-hour. The love and energy that night was very special. In the daylight of the next morning, we were faced with hotel bills, stars' salaries, expenses, plus dozens of other bills, not to mention all the complaints about it not being at the Palladium.

Rocky fans look confused: "Why aren't we at the Palladium?"

The promoter of the event on Halloween night at Roseland came to a temporary rescue and paid necessary bills. He did this simply because he needed the stars for his event which had been well publicized on Radio. Amazingly, these problems didn't hurt ROCKY HORROR because the show did go on and gave the film lots of publicity, but it did have an adverse affect on the fan club group.

Larry, Jude and all the regulars, faced with all the embarrassment and tension and problems of this week, soured toward the fan club organization. They decided to back out of the group because some of them had used their own money to pay bills, for which they were not reimbursed.

Even though the fan club was not financially responsible for the bills, I was devastated by all this because it had the fan club's name on it. As president and leader of the club, I felt morally responsible and tried desperately to keep the club afloat and pay back some of the bills.

Eventually, lawyers for the two producers and the local promoter tried to iron out the problem. Some bills were settled, others to this day have never been paid. Time has a way of making things disappear. I still look back at that experience with a bad taste in my mouth.

NEXT STAGE OF THE FAN CLUB

I found myself at another crossroad. The rest of the officers of the fan club disassociated themselves. Should I do the same? Yet I still loved ROCKY HORROR, the audience participation, and this organization I had worked so hard to build. However, I couldn't do it alone.

Meanwhile, a rival fan club, the International ROCKY HORROR Fan Club, had been started by Adam Sargis of Philadelphia. Adam was more of a business man than a "fan" person. He was interested in merchandising and other business aspects of fandom, while I was a "fan" person with no real desire for the business.

There had been a problem between the two fan clubs, but with Richard O'Brien's advice and blessing the two clubs were able to merge. Since I had a ROCKY HORROR reputation with my appearance in "Fame" and my weekly appearance at the 8th Street Playhouse, I became the President. Adam became the Business Manager of this new organization. That is how the official ROCKY HORROR PICTURE SHOW Fan Club came to be, without a board of directors and all the other things we had been used to.

Adam and I worked together in keeping the fan club going throughout the early 1980's. Under this new regime we printed a Transylvanian supplement and two more Transylvanians, Transylvanian #4 on the release of SHOCK TREATMENT, and what we called the special Transylvanian, on the release of the Audience Participation Album.

Even though Adam and I did not start out as very good friends, working together for <u>ROCKY</u> made us close. Adam no longer has anything to do with the fan club for he is now a successful film editor, but he was instrumental in keeping the fan club alive.

CONVENTIONS

In 1979, 1980 and 1981, I appeared at three Transylvanian conventions in Los Angeles. These conventions were run by Rick Sloane, a young budding filmmaker. Rick really enjoyed <u>ROCKY HORROR</u>, but he seemed to run the conventions as a showcase to exhibit his short films, which were coming attractions for awful horror films such as, <u>Night of The Loving Dead</u> and <u>Clown Whores of Hollywood</u> among others.

Rick's conventions were usually well attended and lots of fun. They included: dealers, tables, costume contests, question and answer sessions, and live performances from local casts. At these conventions, I had a chance to meet some of the great, early West Coast casts. I especially enjoyed meeting the group from the Tiffany on Sunset Boulevard. The last of Rick's conventions in 1981 was in Anaheim, right near Disneyland. I remember going into a Denny's for breakfast and seeing all the stares that the costumed characters got from the straight tourists. They were enough to make Minnie Mouse blush. The convention was held in a big hotel and in an adjoining ballroom was a wedding. It was very funny, later in the afternoon, when I looked in and saw a *Frank-N-Furter* and a *Columbia* dancing among all the formal wear.

This specific convention was right before the releases of SHOCK TREATMENT (the RHPS follow-up, which will be discussed later). So Twentieth Century Fox took advantage of this and had camera crews from the television show "Real People" come to report on the cult and the upcoming film. Of course, instead of being happy that we had a national television report on his convention, Rick was annoyed that it took time away from his short film subjects.

Janets prepare for costume contest at Transylvanian Convention.

In May of 1984, I returned to L.A. for another convention. This time it was in a swanky hotel in Beverly Hills. It was organized by longtime active ROCKY HORROR fans Brian Malion and Megan Harris, who performed with their cast Lipsinc out of the Ken Theater, in San Diego. I persuaded Dori to come out of retirement, for she had not done *Frank* in about 2 years, and come to the convention. At the last minute, Dori had to cancel,

*Costume contest entrants
at Rockycon 84.*

*Sal Timewarps with California
fans on stage of Roxy Theater
where play started in U.S. at
Halloween Party 1983.*

Roxy Halloween Party 1983.

for she was not feeling well. I brought my sister Lillias along to visit California and attend the convention where she actually got to perform live at the show. She sang a medley from SHOCK TREATMENT and "Science Fiction Double Feature" from ROCKY HORROR. Of course I gave my standard talk and slide show presentation that I had given at many colleges. Then I conducted the question and answer period. Plus, I did a special live version of "Toucha-Toucha-Touch-Me," taking my bra and slip out of retirement. It was a well-run convention and everyone had a good time.

Five Frank-N-Furters "strut their stuff" at Rockycon 84.

Dennis Miller poses with a
Magenta at Rockycon 1984.

There was an amusing note in the program: "Proper dress is required when walking through the hotel. This means no corsets, underwear, garters, and fishnet stockings worn openly. Please wear some covering." I guess we were ready for Beverly Hills, but Beverly Hills was not ready for us.

In 1985, there was the biggest convention of all, the 10th anniversary of the ROCKY HORROR PICTURE SHOW. This will be discussed in Chapter Nine.

On July 25, 1986, I had the extreme pleasure of appearing as a special guest at the RHPS five-state convention, covering Michigan, Ohio, Indiana, Illinois and Wisconsin. It was held at the Warren Cinema City in Warren, Michigan. This event was organized by the local cast, "Shock Treatment," that was put together and run by the amazing Hess family of Warren (son Mike as *Frank*, Mom Diane as *Columbia*, daughter Lisa as *Janet* and Dad Gary on lights). This convention was a real party and fun for all. Later it shifted back to the Hess home for

Program from 5 State Convention.

an all-nighter with dozens of ROCKY HORROR regulars from all over the country having a wonderful time.

On Friday evening, August 28, 1987, I drove up to Rochester, New York, with Fan Club assistants Jimmy Colgate and Butch Fields for a ROCKY HORROR convention. This event was run by Eric Bradshaw, editor of Castle Times, and his cast, "Midnight Madness." This was a great time, where we were able to meet fans from New York, Connecticut, Massachusetts and Canada.

On Saturday, March 26, 1988, I was the guest of the Florida Transylvanian convention, sponsored by the Fantasie Factory Players, who held court weekly at the AMC Fashion Village 8 Theater in Orlando. This group was the most organized I had

Flyer for Orlando convention.

ever encountered in all my years at ROCKY HORROR. They had: committees, subcommittees, Friday cast assignments, Saturday cast assignments, lighting directors, meetings, award dinners, press releases. I thought I was visiting General Motors, not a ROCKY HORROR cast. The awards dinner the night before was fun and I met many great ROCKY HORROR fans from Florida.

Sal and Jimmy Colgate with Connecticut fans at Rochester convention.

The next day was the second longest day of my life. (The 10th anniversary being the longest!) We arrived at the hotel ballroom to set up at 9 a.m. for an all-day convention. With dealers, tables, meeting people, the showing of related ROCKY HORROR films, raffles and a costume contest, the all-day convention was finished at 8 o'clock that evening. I had an hour to change and get to their theater for two back-to-back showings of ROCKY HORROR, one at 10 p.m. and the second at 12:45 a.m. Both of these showings included Tim Curry and Meatloaf shorts, my usual preshow announcements and the Fantasie Factory Players' preshow and floor show during the movie. Then, back to the hotel at 3:30 a.m. and up to catch a plane at 7 a.m. What a day! But I loved it. I must say that, even though it was a long day, it was a well organized event thanks to the perseverance of Jeff Cisneros and his cast. Or should I say conglomerate? Jeff was also responsible for putting together a cast directive called "Transylvania University," which I still use for my cast representatives around the country. Unfortunately, since then, Jeff and his group have broken up and years later have been replaced by a new cast. It was a pleasure working with them at the time.

Fans in Orlando.

Photos: Cathy Guidry

Sal visits one of the casts at Cocoa Beach while in Florida.

In June of 1988, I was invited by Gene Chiovari and Tim Miller to a ROCKY HORROR convention at the 400 Theater in Chicago. Gene has been active for many years in ROCKY HORROR as a *Frank-N-Furter*. He is very knowledgeable in ROCKY HORROR history and trivia and is an avid collector. He used to be a member of the Oriental Theater in Milwaukee, but now running the cast in Chicago with his friend Tim Miller, a *Riff Raff*.

At Chicago convention 1988, Sal welcomes Dennis Miller from Los Angeles.

The 400 Theater is huge and the convention included a long preshow of short subjects and preshow numbers, some even live. I got to meet up with many of my old friends from earlier conventions and anniversaries. It was a good time.

The next year, in June of 1989, they repeated their previous success with a second convention. This time, they were able to book Richard O'Brien himself, who came accompanied by his son Linus. This was an exciting time because many of the fans had never seen Richard live and it was a thrill for them to meet him. In fact, Richard spent over two hours giving autographs and taking photos with people.

In June of 1989, Richard O'Brien's
THE ROCKY HORROR SHOW
will be reaching it's 16th birthday
AND WE'RE CELEBRATING ! !

On June 17th, 1989, Albatross Productions will be presenting it's SECOND ANNUAL ANNIVERSARY CELEBRATION for Mr. O'Brien's Sci-Fi Rock Comedy Spoof that has kept us Time Warpin' for all these years!

THIS YEAR OUR TITLE READS:
HAPPY BIRTHDAY DEAR ROCKY
(A SWEET 16 CELEBRATION)

The president of The Official International Rocky Horror Picture Show Fan Club, Mr. Sal Piro, will be returning once again this year to reprise his role as Master of Ceremonies for the festivities. Also, as of the time of this mailout, RICHARD O'BRIEN is tentatively scheduled to appear.

Providing this years entertainment is the 400 Theatre's live floor show cast, Midnight Madness. They will be performing a special tributive preshow commemorating Mr. O'Brien's cult creation.

Along with this special show, Midnight Madness will be hosting a ROCKY HORROR COSTUME CONTEST with a first prize in each category, and a grand prize over all. A special raffle will be held for a very rare pressing of "THE TIME WARP/HOT PATOOTIE" from the movie on a 78RPM RECORD and a FULL SET OF ROCKY HORROR BUBBLE GUM CARDS. This offer is only available to advance ticket buyers only, so be sure to mark the enclosed order form accordingly.

In addition, Albatross Productions and Midnight Madness will be donating LONDON PLAY PACKAGES as FREE DOOR PRIZES for EVERY 69th PERSON who crosses our threshold. This package consists of: copies of a Playbill style advert. for the Original London Cast, London cast button, copy of the original programme, and a copy of the Original London Cast Album.

We will also be showing film shorts from TIM CURRY and MEATLOAF, and a film trailer for THE FIRST NORTH AMERICAN TOUR OF THE ROCKY HORROR SHOW and other surprises.

Richard O'Brien signs autographs at Chicago convention 1989

*Sal and Richard O'Brien
at Chicago convention*

At this second convention, the Chicago cast actually acted out the entire play, complete with music, as a tribute to Richard O'Brien. Good show guys!

As I tell you about these conventions, it is very hard to convey to you the real excitement of being at one, seeing six *Franks* trying to outstrut each other. Fishnets, garter belts, sequins, feather dusters, bald wigs, leather jackets, wheelchairs and gold lamé trunks are all on display. There is a wonderful spirit and that is what I love about the true ROCKY HORROR fans — that mutual love for the film that will forever live in their hearts.

n May of 1979, I received a phone call from Margery Simkin who was the casting director of a new movie. Called "Hot Lunch," about kids at the High School of Performing Arts in New York City, Margery, scouting talented teenagers for the film, wanted to come down to ROCKY HORROR and see our show. The next Saturday night she came with the film's director, Alan Parker, who had directed "Midnight Express" and "Bugsy Malone." Thinking that they might be discovered, most of my cast were pretty nervous, except for me. I knew I was talented, but I was far from being a teenager.

That night as I was doing my usual pre-show warmup and announcements, I had a heckler. Not realizing that our pre-show and my announcements were part of the ritual, he shouted, in a nasty tone, "Get on with the show!" To which I replied, "This is the fuckin' show and if you don't like it you can go see the movie in Staten Island!" (We had heard that there was no pre-show or much audience participation at the RHPS showing in Staten Island.)

At that point, all of the regulars and most of the audience screamed and applauded. Many got up on their feet. The heckler sunk into his seat, never to be heard of again.

A few days later, some of my regulars were asked to come in and read with the director. I was also told that the director wanted to meet with me. When I got to the office, the people in front of me and the people behind me were all looking over scenes with which to audition. I was not given a script and wondered why I was there. When I finally went in, Alan Parker told me he loved the whole idea of audience participation. He had received permission to use the Time Warp scene to show

Sal stands behind Director Alan Parker setting up scene in "Fame."

one of the characters from the new movie (Doris) lose her performing inhibitions in front of an audience at ROCKY HORROR. Alan thought the way I had handled the heckler and the audience's response was one of the greatest pieces of live theater he'd ever seen. He wanted to incorporate my opening speech into the movie as an introduction to the Time Warp sequence. I was in shock. Basically, I would be playing myself in the movie.

At that time a porno film came out called Hot Lunch, so the movie's title was changed to Fame. Many people who saw the film thought that the crew had come and filmed us one Saturday night at the 8th Street Playhouse. But anyone who knows filmmaking is aware that it takes hours to get one shot. In fact, the ROCKY HORROR scenes in Fame which take up about five to six minutes of screen time took us two full working days to shoot. The audience of costumed fans was a mixture of 8th Street regulars (including Dori and my sister, Lillias), neighboring floor shows, and professional actors.

My warmup to the audience included: an announcement of Gail Gold's birthday (she is one of our *Magenta's*), a young lady's 150th time at ROCKY, a warning not to throw food at the screen, and of course, dealing with the heckler.

Doris (Maureen Teefy) and Ralph (Barry Miller), in center, participate in a performance of the ROCKY HORROR SHOW in MGM's "Fame."

I ended my sequence with the usual R-O-C-K-Y cheer. The second part of the scene in Fame shows the audience during the part of ROCKY HORROR where *Brad* and *Janet's* car breaks down in the rain. We see the audience participation leading up to the "Time Warp." As the regulars rush to the screen to dance, Fame's Doris (played by Maureen Teefy) joins them. This represents Doris losing her inhibitions — sort of like one of the themes of ROCKY — fantasy free me!

The release of Fame caused great excitement among all the RHPS fans and regulars. But more importantly, it exposed ROCKY HORROR to a whole new audience. Many new "virgins"came out of curiosity after seeing the scenes in "Fame."

Doris (Maureen Teefy) participates in a performance of the ROCKY HORROR SHOW in MGM's "Fame."

Many people had heard of me and the fan club. Now that I was playing myself, the ROCKY HORROR emcee, in the movie, it certified my position and that of the fan club.

Another interesting side effect from "Fame" is that up until then, the audiences, at least in New York, were basically a

Believe it or not — One Saturday night at the 8th Street Playhouse, one of our cast members celebrated his 75th time seeing ROCKY HORROR. The next weekend, he celebrated his 100th viewing. What he had done was to watch the movie 24 times that week on a bootleg videotape. The cast and I were not amused and refused to recognize his achievement. To this day, we only accept the number of times someone has seen it in a movie theater.

white, Wasp-y audience. With the exposure in this urban, multi-ethnic film, ROCKY was discovered by a whole new group of fans.

"Fame" was not the first film in which our group appeared. A year before, Paul Mazursky was making a movie called "Willie and Phil." This film spans a number of years. In the beginning, the two lead characters meet while coming out of the theater after seeing "Jules and Jim," another cult film. The movie ends many years later with the two of them leaving another showing of the same film, only this time there is a long line of ROCKY HORROR regulars doing the Time Warp, anxiously awaiting their favorite midnight attraction.

Last scene in "Willie & Phil"
passing ROCKY HORROR fans.

Some of the big questions back in the late 1970's, as ROCKY HORROR mania was spreading all over the world, were: "What would happen next?" "Will there be a sequel?" "Will *Frank-N-Furter* rise from the dead?" "Will *Brad* and *Janet* find their clothes?" "Will *Dr. Scott* walk again? . . . in high heels?"

There was a lot of talk about a sequel. It was clear that Tim Curry would not reprise his role as *Frank-N-Furter*, so Richard O'Brien wrote a new adventure for *Brad* and *Janet*. This film was called SHOCK TREATMENT. In SHOCK TREATMENT, *Brad* and *Janet* enter a fast-paced world of quiz shows and media manipulation, surrounded by a new set of bizarre characters. The film takes place inside the "Denton Television Studios" (DTV), which is a society in itself. Plot complications develop when *Brad* and *Janet* are chosen as contestants on the "Marriage Maze," DTV's most popular game show. Bert Schnick, the blind host of "Marriage Maze" delights in having contestants committed to Dentonvale for treatment. *Brad* is committed and attended to by the Dentonvale staff of Cosmo and Nation McKinley (Richard O'Brien and Patricia Quinn) and Nurse Ansalong (Little Nell). Besides these three, the only other returning ROCKY stars were Charles Gray as Judge Ol-

Richard O'Brien poses for photo on set of SHOCK TREATMENT. Barry Humphries in rear.

Pat Quinn on set of SHOCK TREATMENT.

iver Wright and Ralph Hapschatt played by Jeremy Newson. The RHPS creative team of Director Jim Sharman, Set Designer Brian Thomson and Costume Designer Sue Blane also returned for SHOCK TREATMENT. This time around, *Brad* and *Janet* were played by Cliff DeYoung and Jessica Harper. Jessica Harper had a cult following of her own with her appearance in Phantom of the Paradise.

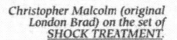

Christopher Malcolm (original London Brad) on the set of SHOCK TREATMENT.

Brian Thomson (Set Designer), Barry Humphries (Burt Schnick) and Jim Sharman (Director) on the set of SHOCK TREATMENT.

When this movie was being filmed, Twentieth Century Fox wanted to promote it by making use of me and the fan club. I was hired to host a documentary entitled "The ROCKY HORROR Treatment." this two-part film traced the development of the ROCKY HORROR cult in anticipation of the sequel, and the actual making of SHOCK TREATMENT. The biggest thrill for me was flying to London to shoot footage on the set of SHOCK TREATMENT. I interviewed the stars of the film and even made a cameo appearance. My "big" role was to stand talking on a telephone behind the staircase in the opening sequence. It was truly an "if you blink, you miss me" role, or "no, that wasn't a speck of dust in your eye, it was me." But I didn't care. That week was the time of my life.

Sal greets Charles Gray on set of SHOCK TREATMENT.

As with <u>ROCKY</u>, this film was tested in a few markets. This was not a movie that could run weekday afternoon shows in a suburban mall and so it was not widely released. It did, however, get spot midnight bookings around the country, and on a few occasions, ran on a double bill with <u>ROCKY HORROR</u>.

Lory Kramer and Betzi Votjko of Oriental in Milwaukee dress in tribute to "SHOCK TREATMENT."

In New York City, while we were firmly implanted at the 8th Street Playhouse, <u>SHOCK TREATMENT</u> was booked Friday and Saturday nights at our old home, the Waverly, just a few blocks away. <u>SHOCK TREATMENT</u> did develop its own floor show and audience participation by a group of fringe people from the Eighth Street Playhouse. They were not very successful and came under much criticism (especially in an article in the Village Voice), by those who said that their participation was forced and not like <u>ROCKY HORROR</u>.

NEW YORK POST, WEDNESDAY, NOVEMBER 4, 1981

On the Town

'Rocky Horror' lovers are in for a 'Shock'

IS THE world ready for a second helping of *Rocky Horror*?

That seems to be the question being mulled both by moviegoers and movie moguls as 20th Century-Fox prepares Friday's release of *Shock Treatment*, the second horrific musical

The Movie Scene
with
ED NABA

spoof penned by Richard O'Brien.

O'Brien, creator of *The Rocky Horror Picture Show*, sums up his latest creation, enigmatically

"It's not a sequel. It's not a prequel. It's an equal."

No one is quite sure whether *Shock Treatment* will be an instant hit, a resounding flop, or a successful flop like its predecessor, the original *Rocky Horror* movie.

Based on O'Brien's semi-successful stage show (it soared in London and L.A., crashed on Broadway), the 1975 *Rocky Horror* film starred Tim Curry as Dr. Frank-n-Furter, a horror film reject who wreaks havoc on the lives of newlywed all-American Brad and Janet.

The film initially bombed, disappearing without ever playing New York. Fox found itself with a film that was D.O.A. instead of S.R.O.

Then, on April 1, 1976, New York's Waverly Theatre began showing the film at midnight. A phenomenon erupted. Repeat audiences flocked to the theater, dressed as their favorite characters and reciting the dialogue during the show.

Fox, seeing a hot property bubbling, encouraged similar mid night madness nationally. The film has now grossed more than $35 million with practically no advertising.

And now comes *Shock Treatment*, a vague sequel with only Brad and Janet surviving the orig inal film. The couple seeks matrimonial counseling on a TV show, *Marriage Maze*, but find themselves trapped by madcap Party Flowers in the TV studio town of Denton, Ohio, instead.

Sound strange? It is, presenting the ultimate contemporary nightmare — a video world filled with omnipresent cameras and talk show hosts.

Carry-overs Jessica Harper and Cliff De Young survive the "Rocky Horror Picture Show" turning up as Janet and Brad in "Shock Treatment" (above) opening Friday at midnight.

Will Frank-n-Furter fans buy this unrelated dementia? No one is taking any chances. Fox hasn't scheduled press screenings so no ad vance word from critics will taint the film's opening. (The show biz newspaper Variety says it a few weeks back and gave it a pretty rocky review.) Fox is hedging its bet further by open ing the first run film at midnights only just in case.

There are some posi tive signs connected with *Shock Treatment's* fate, however. The *Rocky Horror* faithful plan to stand by. Says

Sal Piro, president of the 40,000-member official Rocky Horror Fan Club "I don't think *Shock Treatment* will be more popular than *Rocky Horror* became *Rocky Horror* started it all. It's like Rocky's little brother. It has to be carefully nurtured. You don't want to compare it to the older brother.

"You know, how come you only got a B in school when you're older brother got an A? That's not healthy.

"As long as *Shock Treatment* doesn't wind up with an F, everyone connected with the film will be happy."

53

Closing weekend program for <u>SHOCK TREATMENT</u> floor show at Waverly after 44 performances.

The Eighth Row Players
S H O C K   T R E A T M E N T
Floorshow

Bids Farewell to the Waverly Theatre
After 44 Showings

April 2 & 3, 1982

The Eighth Row Players SHOCK TREATMENT Floorshow Cast
(in order of appearance)

BRAD MAJORS
JANET MAJORS
MACY STRUTHERS
BERT SCHNICK
FARLEY FLAVORS
REST HOME RICKY
DR. COSMO McKINLEY
DR. NATION ...

Mr. Ron Maxwell
Ms. Caryn Essex
Ms. Torie Estes
Mr. Conn M. Quinn
Mr. Charles Stewart
Mr. Lou Knaub
Mr. Robert Madraua
Ms. Violet Falisch
Ms. Peggie Moyer
Mr. Mitchell Wlazlo

Other times.....?)

Row Players Staff***

Conn M. Quinn — Director
Charles Stewart — Ass't. Dir.

Gleich

??
chael Acavallo
han Gleich

rl Turner, and the Staff of the
t Holton, Barry Glasser, Dennis
otions, CMO Associates, DTV
ohn and Holiday, and a big

venue • Brooklyn, New York 11235

Mock Rocky

The line outside the Waverly for the midnight show *Shock Treatment* is reminiscent of those that used to form there for *The Rocky Horror Picture Show*, with a subtle difference. This time the ticket holders are more well behaved, looking like suburban neophytes eager for a place to belong, as if they had seen *Rocky Horror* a few times but had been too shy to penetrate the famed inner fan claque and now hoped to get in on the ground floor of what they'd heard was the long-awaited sequel.

Twentieth Century Fox maintains *Shock Treatment* is not a sequel to *Rocky Horror*, (which is still playing to packed houses at the 8th Street Playhouse), however, since *Shock* has the same producers, director, screenwriter, and composer, as well as several familiar RHPS faces in the cast, it's easy to see why there's some confusion. Even the basic plot structure's the same: sweet young couple caught up in a bizarre universe, this time the game show world of a place or state of mind called Denton.

The couple participates in the game show, he (Cliff de Young, of *Rocky*) somewhat reluctantly, and with good reason, because she (apple-faced Jessica Harper) feels to decline would be disrespectful of the blind, crazy, horrible emcee and of the weirdness that is Denton itself. Though the "show" takes place in a TV-like studio, there doesn't appear to be any outside world; even when de Young gets hauled off to a sanitorium (we never really understand why), which is really a spacoid loony bin where he's straitjacketed into a wheelchair and left drugged in a circular cell, all that action somehow is inside Denton too. The message is clear: Denton is the whole cosmos where inanity is the norm, as is the programmed personality of every citizen of that dreamlike town.

On this last point, the movie steers off course if its intention is to foster a clone of *The Rocky Horror Picture Show* cult. In that epic there was room for the audience to be smart, balanced as it was between the super-naive couple in danger and the extravagant crazies all around them. But in *Shock Treatment* there is no such room. To be smart is to leave early.

Many of the *RHPS* regulars do attend, like the immense redhead who used to dress as an s&m parlormaid and the assortment of other unique specimens all seemingly on intimate terms with each other, but at *Shock Treatment* they group together in side seats, chatting throughout the movie in bored detachment. And these are the people who used to follow every word, gesture, nuance in *Rocky Horror*, dance in aisles, tote crazy props in from New Jersey, duplicate the outlandish screen costumes, and overall put on quite a show themselves. Now they look hired, as (paid to show up just to titillate the folks buying tickets, tricking them into thinking they're about to see a cult in action.

After fashioning acts around *Rocky Horror* that alone made the price of a ticket worthwhile, these part-time freaks without question have won the right to a minor midnight-show-circuit celebrity. As such they also have a right to be disgusted with *Shock Treatment* in which the game show audience blatantly mocks them, as it idiotically feigns fervent, sing-along devotion to the dopeyness of Denton.

Everyone must be part of the act is the precarious rock *Shock Treatment* tries to rest on; the horror is one of gross audience manipulation. To participate in the flesh and make a *Rocky Horror* show out of *Shock Treatment* is unfortunately to join Denton, which doesn't look like fun at all.

Village Voice on <u>SHOCK TREATMENT</u> regulars.

Many <u>ROCKY</u> fans, as myself, loved <u>SHOCK TREATMENT</u>, the music, the characters, the satire. Even though I have seen it only twenty times ("only" becomes a relative word here), I have never felt compelled to yell a single line back at it.

<u>SHOCK TREATMENT</u> is performed in front of the screen by Lori Rice and the "Grove" cast in Miami.

Australian fans dress up as their favorite
SHOCK TREATMENT characters.

SHOCK TREATMENT didn't last very long at the Waverly or
any other theaters and has since been released on videotape.
But it is still a fond piece of ROCKY HORROR history to its
many fans that have experienced "a bit of oooooh SHOCK
TREATMENT!"

Cisco Adler, Lou Adler and Daryl Hannah attending the
10th Anniversary celebration of the ROCKY HORROR
PICTURE SHOW

Photo: Jean C. Pigozzi

One of the requests I most often received at the RHPS fan club was for a script to the audience participation lines. Over the years, many people would send me their own private scripts. Some of the problems were that the verbal responses were so different from region to region or even theater to theater and that new lines were always replacing old ones. Yet it would still have been nice to have some sort of record of this phenomenon. Then, in 1983, Lou Adler called and told me he had this idea to record an audience participation album with the whole soundtrack of the movie complete with audience verbal responses.

I quickly began to compile a script of what I thought were the best responses, the most interesting and the ones that would be understood by everyone. I tried to eliminate private theater in-jokes. I also did not include any lines that were prompted by a physical action, such as "Kick it," because this was a recording. Then I was told to invite two-hundred ROCKY HORROR fans to a recording studio to spend the afternoon shouting these lines on cue. It became a big party/ROCKY event, with refreshments and each person receiving a copy of the now very rare and valuable ROCKY HORROR picture disk. It was a long, hectic, but fun afternoon, working with so many fans and directing them to shout all this "counterpoint dialogue" on cue. Louis Farese, the first RHPS fan to shout at the screen, would have been proud.

For the next step, I flew to California to work with the record's producer, Howard Frank, and a sound editor to get the timing

"Say It!"

Clipping on *Audience Participation Album* from *Calendar* — *L.A. Times*.

perfect on the insertion of these responses into the soundtrack of the film. That week, we must have listened to that soundtrack close to one-hundred times. When it was completed, it was technically perfect, but the end result did not sound spontaneous. Lou felt that it sounded phony and contrived, almost as if it were two-hundred people shouting in a studio. So, the next step was to come back to New York to the 8th Street Playhouse and actually record the whole night at the theater and get actual audience responses and sounds while the film was going on.

They did this on a Friday, and again on a Saturday night. The end result was the recording we have today. Cherished by thousands of fans around the world, it is actually an incredible mix of those two nights and the studio recording session.

Another highlight for me was that I played the emcee at the beginning of the album. My favorite part of the record was a last minute brainstorm. At the end of the album, I was the lone voice who says, "You mean its over? I gotta go home? You're not gonna show it again?"

In early 1985, I was uncertain about the future of ROCKY HORROR and the fan club and my involvement. Adam Sargis became more involved in film editing and basically stepped back from the fan club. I was now taking on all the duties of the club by myself and was running out of merchandise and the premiums that were provided to members for their membership fees, which were supporting the fan club and keeping it alive. I did not have the capital to produce new items for these members.

I wasn't totally alone — I did get some assistance with my mailing work over the years. I will forever be indebted to my three most capable assistants, affectionately known as "The Inner Circle." They included: Kathy Fountain, David "Butch" Fields, and Jimmy Colgate, who played *Rocky* at the 8th Street Playhouse for over six years.

The tenth anniversary of the release of the film was approaching and I had hoped that there would be some sort of celebration. Lou Adler called and said they were planning a big event for the anniversary. What was very lucky for us was that Tim Deegan, the ad executive who was responsible for getting ROCKY HORROR booked at the Waverly, had returned to Twentieth Century Fox as a vice president. We now had one of ROCKY HORROR's biggest allies at the studio, which made the planning of the anniversary that much easier.

I went to L.A. to meet with Tim Deegan, Lou Adler and Fox executives for the big planning session. Even though the actual anniversary is in late September, it was mutually agreed upon that we would celebrate it on Halloween since that day is always considered our national holiday.

Lots of cities were considered, but it was agreed that New York City was best because it is always the center of media attention, the home of the fan club and where the audience participation had begun.

Many venues to hold the event were discussed, including Radio City Music Hall, which was unfortunately booked on Halloween. It was finally decided that the anniversary would be at the Beacon Theater, a 3000 seat concert hall on 74th Street and Broadway in Manhattan.

There was so much to do and our number one priority was to book as many of the original cast of the movie as possible. Barry Bostwick, Susan Sarandon, and Meatloaf reside in the United States and were easily reached through their agents. The rest of the cast were British. Richard O'Brien (*Riff Raff*), Jonathan Adams (*Dr. Scott*), and Pat Quinn (*Magenta*), veterans of past conventions, accepted our invitation. Charles Gray, who had only spent two days filming his role as the *criminologist* and never really interacted with the rest of the cast, was not interested in attending. Peter Hinwood (*Rocky*) was nowhere to be found. Richard told me that he hadn't seen him in years. (Many rumors floated around about his supposed death, but the most recent rumor that he is an antique dealer is true.)

DID YOU KNOW . . .

In Tim Curry's video of the song "Paradise Garage," the *Frank-N-Furter* who does a quick crossover past Tim is our very own Dori Hartley?

☆　☆

The original title of THE ROCKY HORROR PICTURE SHOW (the play) was They Came From Denton High? Next it was changed to The Rocky Horror Show.

☆　☆

The original opening of RHPS was not the lips? It was a montage of photos from all the science fiction films mentioned in the opening song "Science Fiction, Double Feature."

10th Anniversary flier.

Little Nell had left England and moved back to her native Australia. I tracked her down through a series of phone calls and she agreed to come from "Down Under" for the celebration. (In fact, Nell never returned to Australia except for visits. She stayed in New York City after the 10th Anniversary and, with some old friends, opened the nightclub "Nell's," which became one of the elite watering holes of the rich and famous in the late 80's.)

Tim Curry, who had attended few ROCKY HORROR events, wanted to attend, but the event fell on the day of the final dress rehearsal for a play he was doing at the National Theater in London and he couldn't come. So, we were able to get seven of ten of the original cast. Not bad.

The planning and publicizing of the event took months of hard work. Advance notice was sent to the fan club members throughout the country and they were offered the first choice of seats in the center up front. The first two tickets sold through the club came from Topeka, Kansas. (Gee, Toto, we're not in Transylvania anymore!) Orders came from all over the country. Carpools and buses came from as far as California and two young ladies flew in from London just for the anniversary.

A special poster/program cover was designed — a photo of a huge anniversary cake with dolls dressed as the characters from the movie placed on the cake's tiers. It was beautiful, but this poster/program cover was pulled back at the last minute. It seemed that Ken and Barbie dolls, or a reasonable facsimile, were used in the photo and Fox's legal department feared reprisal from Mattel. New program covers were made with the usual "lips" logo. Today, those original posters are very valuable on the collectors' market.

Three weeks before the event, a big media blitz began. Local, national and even international, newspapers, magazines and publications all clamored for stories and interviews. Some of the best were in <u>Time</u>, <u>USA Today</u>, <u>Newsweek</u>, and <u>New York Magazine</u>. And there was television — the actual day of the event there seemed to be more TV cameras than fans — with very interesting stories on CNN cable network news, USA cable's <u>Night Flight</u>, <u>Entertainment Tonight</u>, the CBS morning program, and <u>NBC Nightly News</u> with Tom Brokaw.

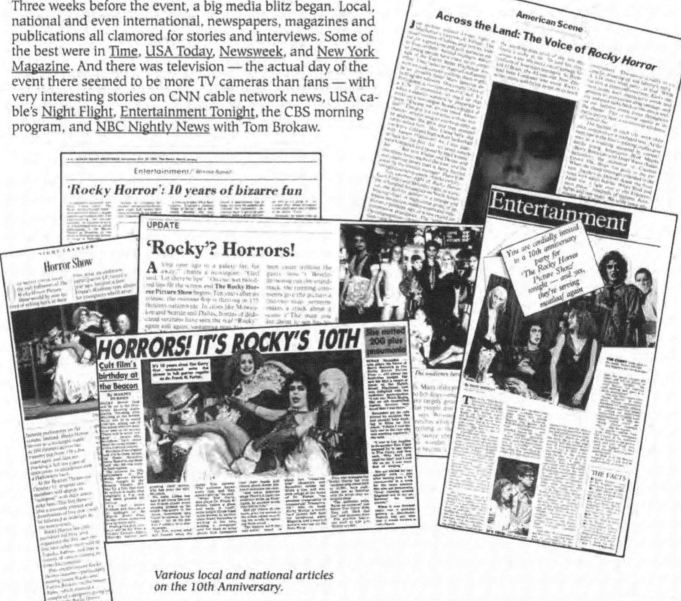

Various local and national articles on the 10th Anniversary.

A lot of these stories and articles keyed in on how many times I had seen the film (853 at the time). All this publicity later led to me being inducted into the <u>Guinness Book of World Records</u>.

Ticket sales were very slow initially, but once all the publicity hit, the Beacon Theater on Halloween became the hottest ticket in town. We were sold out and I even heard the scalpers were getting $100 a ticket on the street.

My day began at six a.m. I was live on the radio on K-Rock, one of New York's local rock stations, doing an interview and taking phone calls. Then I was transported to CBS Studios where I did a live national interview on <u>CBS This Morning</u>, with Richard O'Brien and Barry Bostwick. What I most remember from that interview was when Richard O'Brien described <u>ROCKY HORROR</u> as a film about the loss of innocence, kind of a <u>Babes in the Woods</u> story or an updated Hansel and Gretel story. Then when Barry Bostwick was asked about his character he said that *Brad* starts out as Hansel, but ends up as Gretel. From that interview, I went directly to the Beacon to prepare for the night's festivities. There were

Did you know — back at one of the early *ROCKY HORROR* conventions in 1978 on Long Island, a local band played during intermission? Nobody paid much attention to that band called "Twisted Sister."

Program inserts.

programs to be collated, the setting up of the band, rehearsal of live acts and fans to meet and greet from all over the country. Looking back, that whole day was like one big blur to me. I don't think I ever sat down or stopped talking.

The doors opened at six o'clock that evening and for the next two hours there was posing and strutting and photo taking and plenty of excitement. The show began at eight o'clock. First was a set of short videos and trailers: Tim Curry's "I Do the Rock" and "Paradise Garage," Meatloaf's "Bat Out of Hell" and "Paradise by the Dashboard Light," the "Megaforce" trailer with Barry Bostwick, the clip from "Fame," and finally, "The Contraption," a short film with Richard O'Brien, where a man builds a huge "contraption" that turns out to be a giant mousetrap and ends with him releasing it onto himself. The last film shown was the not-often-seen preview trailer to ROCKY HORROR.

Then, Ron Maxwell, one of the best *Brad Majors* I've ever seen, came on the stage, accompanied by hundreds of people chanting "asshole," in deference to his character. He introduced me and I came out in a beautiful ROCKY HORROR T-shirt that Richard O'Brien had brought from London. On that stage, I did most of my preshow announcements that I was known for, but only a grander scale. I welcomed all the special guests in the audience, making special note of all the casts that had flown in from all over the country. Then I welcomed my special guest, a woman whose two children had seen ROCKY HORROR over 1400 times — my mother. As I introduced her, it was a funny sight to see this sweet older woman stand up among all these costumed fans. Then I led the traditional ROCKY cheer — the crowd was filled with great antici — SAY IT! — pation for the introduction of the stars.

As each "Star" was introduced, many people rushed to the front of the stage from their seats. Ushers with microphones were stationed in the audience for a question and answer period many

Mrs. Eileen Piro watches her son lead 3000 people in cheers.

Photo: Bob Klein

*Katz (second from left) and the gang
from Montreal are introduced.*

Photo: Bob Klein

fans finally able to get answers to those queries that they had longed to ask.

After this, we awarded mock Oscars to all the stars for their performances that had been overlooked by the Academy. The final Oscar was given to Richard O'Brien for "Best Picture." Backstage, Lou Adler presented a mock oscar to Angelica Huston thus forecasting the oscar she would win for "Prizzi's Honor." Richard read a telegram from producer Michael White, sending his regrets for not being there. Then, the original cast left the stage to prepare for the live numbers.

With the absence of Tim Curry, I came up with a unique way to stage a performance of "Sweet Transvestite." I had five of our

*Pat Quinn, Richard O'Brien and
Little Nell answer questions.*

Photo: Bob Klein

8th Street Playhouse *Frank-N-Furters* lipsynch a group version of the number. It was very well received.

Next there was a special treat for everyone — after being out of ROCKY HORROR for almost four years, Dori Hartley came out of retirement and, dressed as *Frank*, sang "I'm Going Home" live. She sounded so much like Tim Curry that people in the back of the audience swore that she was lipsynching.

And then, out rolled Jonathan Adams in a wheelchair, who to the delight of the crowd, sang "Eddie's Teddy." He was followed by Meatloaf singing "Hot Patootie." But the real big treat was that while the number was going on, Susan Sarandon and Little Nell came out and sang backup. And then the number everyone was waiting for — Richard O'Brien, Pat Quinn and Little Nell doing the "Time Warp."

After this, there was a costume contest that was judged by the stars of the film. They were amazed at how much so many of the people looked exactly like the characters in the film.

Sal awards Richard O'Brien a 'mock' Oscar for Best Picture.

Photo: Bob Klein

Dori Hartley belts out "I'm Going Home."

Photo: Bob Klein

After the contest, while everyone prepared for the finale, I came up with an idea for a comedy sketch, *Janet Weiss* on the Dating Game. The three bachelors that *Janet* (Jennifer Whitney) interviewed for a date were: *Frank-N-Furter* (Brendan Conboy), *Brad* (Ron Maxwell) and *Rocky* (Jimmy Colgate).

The finale was a full cast version of the song "Little Black Dress" from SHOCK TREATMENT. Each person had a new verse, written by Richard especially for them, as they came out. Richard sang "Science Fiction" and the whole house was in awe. Then there was a full cast reprise of the "Time Warp." It was a live show that everyone in the theatre room would remember for a very long time. To top the evening, the reason for the celebration, the ROCKY HORROR PICTURE SHOW, was shown at midnight, complete with the 8th Street floorshow.

Looking back at the first ten years, in the program I dedicated the anniversary show to the five men I consider responsible for everything we did there that night: to Richard O'Brien, the

8th Street "Rocky" — Jimmy Colgate poses with the real Brad — Barry Bostwick.

man whose perverted pen brought us the music, lyrics, story, and wonderful characters to which we have become so attached; to Michael White, the British producer, who had the guts and insight to produce THE ROCKY HORROR SHOW on the usually conservative British stage; to Lou Adler, the American producer, who had the guts and insight to bring ROCKY HORROR to American audiences and who has exercised creative control in the marketing of the film as he does to this day; to Tim Deegan, the Twentieth Century Fox executive, who knew audiences would love this movie and gave us our midnight party; to Tim Curry, whose memorable portrayal of *Dr. Frank-N-Furter* will stay in our hearts and minds for a very long time; and, lastly, this night is for all of us, the fans who have remained devoted to *Dr. Frank-N-Furter* and his cohorts through all these years.

10th Anniversary trivia quiz and answers.

After the great success of the tenth Anniversary and its surrounding publicity, the fan club's mail increased. I was now out of most of the premiums and merchandise that I provided with membership. It was basically a one-man operation, and I really had no desire to continue in the business aspects of running a fan club. Everyone was very pleased with the anniversary's success and my participation, so with the help of Tim Deegan, I was able to persuade the studio to support the business end of the fan club. My reasoning behind this was that, unlike a rock band's fan who might have one album and possibly two concerts to attend a year, a ROCKY HORROR fan has fifty-two weekends to attend, plus the costumes, makeup and props if they perform. I thought it would be proper if we made the fan club free. For a self-addressed stamped envelope, all interested parties receive a membership card, a fan club button, and a newsletter with up-to-date information of the movie and its stars. Also, they are put on the national mailing list for new products, and they can have their fan mail forwarded to the stars. More importantly, I like to answer all questions and special requests from fans around the world.

Welcome letter sent to new members.

THE ROCKY HORROR PICTURE SHOW OFFICIAL FAN CLUB
204 West 20th Street, New York City, NY 10011

THE ROCKY HORROR FAN CLUB IS FREE AND OPEN TO ALL.
SEND A SELF-ADDRESSED STAMPED ENVELOPE TO THE
ABOVE ADDRESS.

****

ROCKY HORROR NEWS FALL/WINTER 1989

TOP STORY: ROCKY HORROR is no longer playing at the 8th Street Playhouse in New York City. Sal Piro and company will now be at the Eastside Cinema at 55th Street and Third Avenue. Jessica Harper (SHOCK TREATMENT's Janet) is a regular on "The Gary Shandling Show"....Richard O'Brien is currently the host of a new British game show "The Crystal Maze"....Mr. and Mrs. Richard O'Brien gave birth to a baby girl, Amelia, in January....Susan Sarandon and Tim Robbins gave birth to a baby boy, Jack Henry....Congratulations....Richard O'Brien has created a new rock and roll character "Mephistopheles Smith" and hopes to film a performance video soon....A & M Records has released Tim Curry's Greatest Hits....In June Richard O'Brien and Fan Club President Sal Piro appeared at a convention at Chicago's 400 Theater. Thanks to Tim, Gene and the cast for a great time....Susan Sarandon will be playing a spicy-tongued waitress in The White Palace....Jim Sharman is directing the Australian stage version of "Chess"....Susan Sarandon is featured in the film "A Dry White Season"....Barry Bostwick is a regular on Disney's "Parent Trap III"....Meatloaf will be releasing a new album (Bat out of Hell II)....Tim Curry's "Pass the Ammo" is available on video....Richard O'Brien reports there will be a major revival of The Rocky Horror Show in London in March or April 1990 produced by the original London Brad Christopher Malcolm....Barry Bostwick won a Golden Globe Award for Best Supporting Actor for "War and Remembrance"....For your information the birth dates of the RHPS stars: Jon Adams 2/14, Barry Bostwick 2/24, Richard O'Brien 3/25, Tim Curry 4/19, Nell 5/24, Pat Quinn 5/28, Charles Gray 8/28, Susan Sarandon 10/4, Meatloaf 9/27....To answer the four most asked questions of the fan club: 1) there are no immediate plans to release RHPS on videotape in the U.S.; 2) RHPS costumes are not available in stores. Most theater performers make their own, 3) the "lips" belong to Patricia Quinn (voice by Richard O'Brien) and 4) No one really knows what happened to Peter Hinwood. Rumor has it that he is an antique dealer in England .....There will be a 1990 Rocky Horror calendar available later this year....Very special thanks to Betzi Vojtko for all her years of hard work, service and dedication to ROCKY HORROR. After 100 issues, Betzi has retired as editor of ROCKY HORROR SHOPTALK and the fanzine will no longer be in print. We'll miss you, Betzi....For info on a new ROCKY HORROR Fanzine, send a sase to The Master's Affair, 76-05 Bristol Lane, Unit F, Hanover Park, Illinois 60103....For information on ROCKY HORROR photos, send a sase to Jerry Ohlinger's Movie Material Store, 242 West 14th Street, New York, New York 10014 (Ask for list "37")....For info on the Rocky Horror Trivia Book send a self-addressed stamped envelope to: Mike Hess P.O. Box 292, Fraser, MI 48026....Rhino Records is now releasing all the ROCKY HORROR soundtracks. A new 12" dance version of the "Time Warp" has been released.

Samples of ROCKY HORROR news sent to members.

One of the ways that the Fan Club stays in touch with the theater casts is through the representative system. Dedicated fans, who are regulars or cast members at their local theaters, are appointed Fan Club Representatives (Reps). The main functions of the Reps are to inform people about the Fan Club and to recruit members. It is extrememly difficult to keep in touch with each and every member as we are presently at 15,000 active members. So I contact the Reps to tell them the latest news and happenings and let them pass it on to their club membership.

Letter and application sent to Fan Club 'Rep' applicants.

REPRESENTATIVE INFORMATION SHEET

Please fill out all parts _____ tely and correctly. Print or type.

NAME

ZIP

BER ( )

or Picture Show? _____
vities? _____

THE ROCKY HORROR PICTURE SHOW OFFICIAL FAN CLUB
204 West 20th Street, New York City, NY 10011

Dear Fan Club "Rep" Applicant:

Welcome to the second decade of decadence!! The success of the *RHPS* 10th Anniversary has spawned the all-new improved fan club. With your help, we can celebrate the twentieth anniversary. There will no longer be a $10.95 entrance fee into the fan club. *New members will be accepted for a self-addressed stamped business envelope.* For this they will recieve a button, a membership card, newsletter and info about forwarding mail to the stars and about *RHPS* merchandise for sale. They will be placed on a national mailing list so they will be informed of any new products or *RHPS* events. **IT IS YOUR JOB TO RECRUIT NEW MEMBERS!** You can give out the Fan Club address for them to send in their S.A.S.E.s directly-- or you can collect stamps (or 25 cents) from them and prepare the S.A.S.E.s yourself-- or whatever method you find best. I will have special gifts for those "reps" who recruit the most members. You can also have a 20% discount on all merchandise sold through the fan club.

As a "rep" you can recreate within your own theatre structure the role I have played at the Waverly Theatre and the 8th Street Playhouse in New York City (as seen in the motion picture FAME.) For Rocky Horror to be successful within the theatre, it is always important to keep the enthusiasm going for the regulars and the audience (even the "virgins.") There should never be any jealosy or fighting within the "floorshow" -- you should all be there for the same purpose. If possible, you or someone else should "do announcements" to welcome "virgins," celebrate birthdays and anniversaries, etc. Have running jokes with the audience and develop the personalities of the regulars as part of the show's attraction.

Make people want to come back. This is not to say we are taking anything away from the film and the experience-- rather we are enhancing the experience. Special events could be planned, such as "Bring Your Mom to Rocky Night" or Bring a Virgin to Rocky Night." Also, the theatre anniversary should be special.

If you can fulfill the duties of a rep as listed above AND if you regularly attend a theatre that shows Rocky, then fill out the enclosed form. If you have any special needs or requests, you can write me at the above address.

With absolute pleasure,

Sal Piro, President

on FRI of SAT?

eek?

or Picture Show
lub

oll

The bulk of the letters that I receive ask about the availability of <u>ROCKY HORROR</u> merchandise and where they can purchase it. The collecting of everything related to the film has become a big hobby of many of the fans. Over the years, a great deal of memorabilia has been produced, such as: T-shirts, posters, buttons, greeting cards, calendars, magazines, trading cards, poster magazines, "Lips" pins, banners, books, and even a foto-novel. Most of the original merchandise from the Seventies and Early Eighties is out of print and commands a high price on the collector's market. I worked on the development and creation of many of these products and even contributed materials to some.

ROCKY HORROR trading cards.

Poster magazines.

Some of the letters are filled with panic over the fact that ROCKY HORROR no longer plays at the local theater; or the fans or casts writing may be having problems with the management of their theater. Some of the letter writers are bursting with happiness and excitement over their discovery of ROCKY HORROR and their new found devotion to it.

Some correspondents are curious about the whereabouts or even marital status of the film's stars. All the letters are different. Yet, underneath, the feeling they convey is always the same. "I love ROCKY HORROR." They certainly are a fun group with whom to correspond. I love the fans who name themselves after the characters — out there is a *Riff Raff* Smith, a *Columbia* Jones, and a *Magenta* Abramowitz.

ARTWORK

Even though Dori Hartley was our original Artist-in-Residence of the fan club, she is not the only person to express talent and pay homage to the movie and its characters through art. Over the years, I have received many pieces of artwork from fan club members all around the world. Some are very serious, some are comical, while others are primitive or amateurish. Yet, all are sincere. Many fans draw dripping red letters on the envelope, or they draw huge lips over the letter seal. Here are, reproduced, some of my favorites.

Frank-N-Furter and Riff Raff by Doug Hazelwood of Victoria, Texas.

Homemade RHPS dolls by Maureen Cox of Pennsylvania, 1979.

By Susan Kricorian of Watertown, Mass., 1980.

C. H. Burnett, 1980.

By Dori Hartley.

THE ROCKY HORROR
PICTURE SHOW

Riff-Raff by C. Taylor, 1988.

Frank-N-Furter portrait by Kathy Hembree.

THE NIGHT STUFF

How a culture began.

Betzi Votjko was not only Shoptalk editor but an incredible artist as well.

Artwork by Cortina Bandalero (R.I.P.).

he truly amazing thing about <u>ROCKY HORROR</u> is that this phenomenon is not limited to big urban communities, such as, New York City, L.A., San Francisco. <u>ROCKY HORROR</u> has spread all over. The second midnight booking, just three weeks after the Waverly opened in late April of 1976, was in Austin, Texas, at the Riverside Twin Cinemas, where it ran for years. From that booking, <u>ROCKY HORROR</u> became very popular all over Texas (Cowboy hats and fishnets?). One of the largest continuous runs is at the Graceland Cinema in Columbus, Ohio.

Betzi Vojtko.

ott Mazarin as Frank-N-Furter's cousin,
nock-N-Wurst.

Photo: Lapidus

ROCKY HORROR makes the
"Garbage Pail Kids"

Within weeks Dori's make-up and costumes
improved greatly.

Dori Hartley and her "court" of Waverly regulars in a studio shoot.

Dori and early 8th Street cast, 1979

Photo: P. Pouridas

Cast of Baker St. Cinema in London —
Charming Underclothes.

Photo: David Freeman

Cover of *Transylvanian #3*, rarest
of fan club magazines.

Sal and Eastside Cinema cast.   Photo: Teddy Sexton

*Cincinnati cast Denton Affair
at Skywalk Cinema.*

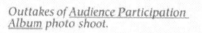
Outtakes of <u>Audience Participation Album</u> photo shoot.

Photos of 10th anniversary at Beacon Theater, N.Y.C., Oct. 31, 1985.

Photos: Bob Klein

The original cake poster of 10th anniversary.

Jonathan Adams rocks the house with "Eddie's Teddy."

Richard O'Brien presents Little Nell with "mock" Oscar.

Barry Bostick and Susan Sarandon together again.

Richard O'Brien acknowledges crowd's ovation.

Pat Quinn, Richard O'Brien and Little Nell answer questions.

Meatloaf makes grand entrance.

Sal emcees the 10th anniversary show.

Sal, Lillias, Barbara and Todd Pose with Japanese floorshow at Cinemarise Theater in Tokyo, July, 1988.

Japanese poster, 1988.

3ʳᵈ ANNUAL

MUSIC! GUESTS! FUN!

ROCKY HORROR

BIRTHDAY PARTY & COSTUME BALL
CASH PRIZES FOR BEST COSTUMES

Live stage performance by
"THE ROCKY HORROR REVIEW"
April 28 at 8:00 p.m. • PARAMOUNT THEATRE
TICKETS - $4.50-$5.50-$6.50 available at the Riverside Twin,
Village Cinema Four, Lakehills Cinema Four and Dobie Screens

THE DAILY TEXAN
Wednesday, April 25, 1979
Page 13

AUSTIN'S 11ᵀᴴ BIRTHDAY PARTY

FOR

The Rocky Horror Picture Show

NORTHCROSS 6 THEATRES
MAY 8-9, 1987

MIDNITE SHOW

FRIDAY & SATURDAY
Starting JUNE 2nd & 3rd

THE ROCKY HORROR PICTURE SHOW

a different kind of ROCKY.

NC NO CANDLES   SEPARATE ADMISSION - $2.00

UA STATE, Jersey City
2854 KENNEDY BOULEVARD • 653-5200

DISCO 96

IS PROUD TO PRESENT
A SPECIAL HALLOWEEN SHOWING OF

THE ROCKY HORROR PICTURE SHOW
R

Wednesday, October 31st
Doors Open 7:00 P.M.
Prizes & Surprises 7:30 P.M.
Rocky Horror Film 8:00 P.M.

Grove Cinema
3199 Grand Avenue / Coconut Grove

HOLD THIS NUMBER
FOR FABULOUS PRIZES!

**PLEASE ADMIT ONE
THIS SHOW
ONLY**

81

Every Saturday at Midnight

2ND ANNIVERSARY PARTY

THE ROCKY HORROR PICTURE SHOW

Grove Cinema 3199 Grand Ave., Coconut Grove, Fl

SCIENCE FICTION REIGNS
at
THE COSTUME HOUSE

Costume Rentals— Makeup — Accessories
8200 ½ Menaul NE Upstairs
268-1206 Hoffmantown Westend

THE ROCKY HORROR PICTURE SHOW featuring The Celluloid Jam
ORIENTAL THEATRE, MILWAUKEE

Los Angeles has always been a big ROCKY HORROR town. In the late 1970's, the Tiffany Theater on Sunset Boulevard was the "8th Street Playhouse" of the West. It was so popular that they would run a midnight show and a 2 a.m. show on Fridays and Saturdays. One of the first well-known West Coast performers as *Dr. Frank-N-Furter* was Michael Wolfson, who ran the ROCKY HORROR Revue that played in many California theaters, including the Tiffany. The Tiffany is no longer a movie house and now the big L.A. group is at the Nu-Art Theater. This group is brought together by fan club Rep Dennis Miller.

Cast members of Tiffany Theater in Los Angeles, 1979.

Fan Club Rep. Erik Kellstrom and Los Angeles regulars march in annual Doo-Dah Parade, 1989.

Time Warp instructions signed by Andy Warhol in lobby of Tiffany, Los Angeles, 1979.

Michael Wolfson and first Los Angeles cast — The ROCKY HORROR Revue, 1977.

Michael Wolfson, 1977

Early national article in Circus Magazine about Michael Wolfson and Tiffany cast. The article tells of a real ROCKY HORROR wedding.

Nuart in Los Angeles before, during and after "ROCKY HORROR".

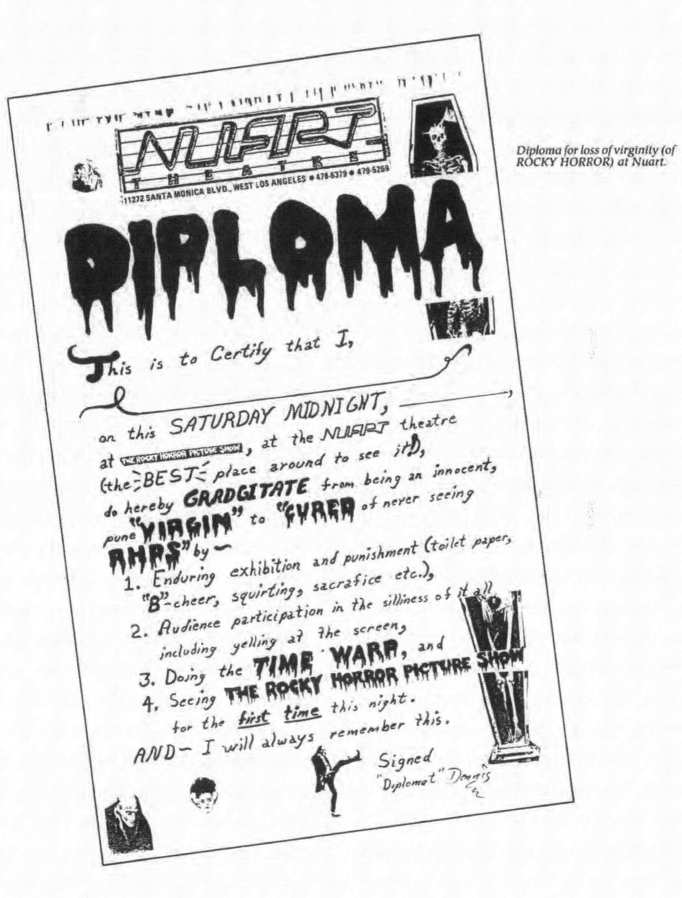

Diploma for loss of virginity (of ROCKY HORROR) at Nuart.

The reigning group in San Francisco in the late 70's was Double Feature at the Strand with Marni Scofidio and company. They were very jealous of 8th Street's reputation and actually issued a challenge to us in a newspaper article for a floor show showdown. (I always found such rivalries petty and filled with jealousy for no reason. After all, we are all in this because we love <u>ROCKY HORROR</u>. Leave the green-eyed monster home.)

Columbia of Double Feature cast San Francisco 1979 passes the hat.

The Grove Cinema in Miami has been showing <u>ROCKY HOR-ROR</u> since 1977. They had a huge second anniversary party that actually had guest appearances by Richard O'Brien and Little Nell.

Fan Club "Rep" Lori Rice wears dozens of RHPS buttons with pride.

THE ROCKY HORROR PICTURE SHOW Featuring ROCK CANDY the official cast of the Grove Cinema

Richard O'Brien signs autographs at Grove's second anniversary party.

The Oriental Theater in Milwaukee, Wisconsin is one of the pioneering <u>ROCKY HORROR</u> theaters in the country and the longest running in the Midwest. The <u>ROCKY HORROR PICTURE SHOW</u> began its landmark run there in 1978 and is still going strong today. Within its history, the Oriental has hosted many great <u>ROCKY</u> parties, presented many floor shows, and

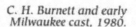

C. H. Burnett and early Milwaukee cast, 1980.

Gene Chiovari (Frank), Betzi Vojtko (Magenta), and Bruce Cutter (Riff) head the Celluloid Jam of the mid 80's.

even had a surprise visitor, Meatloaf, who reportedly stopped by after one of his early Milwaukee concerts. The Oriental Theater was also the home of <u>Shoptalk</u>, the longest running <u>ROCKY HORROR</u> fanzine in the country. It is now the base for <u>The Master's Affair</u> a truly fitting follow-up to <u>Shoptalk</u>. The house cast at the Oriental is the Celluloid Jam, performing at midnight on Saturdays.

*The Celluloid Jam today —
still as popular as ever.*

*Tom Schaefer (Riff Raff) —
editor of The Master's Affair
poses at Oriental.*

The 12th Anniversary of

The Rocky Horror Picture Show

January 27th at midnight

Oriental Theatre
at the corner of **North** and **Farwell**
Milwaukee, WI.   (414)276-8711

The Celluloid Jam
CAST APPLICATION

NAME _____

ADDRESS _____   OLD LADY NAME _____

PHONE( ) _____ STREET _____ CITY _____ STATE ___ ZIP __

ARE YOU EMPLOYED? _____ BIRTHDAY _____

CAN YOU BE HERE EVERY SATURDAY NIGHT? _____

DO YOU HAVE YOUR OWN TRANSPORTATION? _____

DO YOU HAVE ANY DRAMATIC EXPERIENCE? _____ OR ACCESS TO? _____

DO YOU HAVE ANY STAGE CRAFT (LIGHTING, SOUND, PROPS) EXPERIENCE? _____

WHY ARE YOU INTERESTED IN JOINING THE CAST? _____

DO YOU HAVE A COSTUME? _____ WHICH CHARACTER(S)? _____

ARE YOU WILLING TO PUT A COSTUME TOGETHER IF A PART BECOMES AVAILABLE? _____

ARE YOU WILLING TO DO LIGHTING IF NO PARTS ARE AVAILABLE? _____

WHAT CAST JOB/POSITION DO YOU PREFER? _____

CAN YOU BE AVAILABLE FOR SPECIAL FRIDAY NIGHT OR SA_____
REHEARSALS? _____

SPECIAL TALENTS _____

The Celluloid Jam

1986

See **ROCKY HORROR** At The **ORIENTAL**
Milwaukee's ORIGINAL Rocky Theatre

ROCKY HORROR has always been hot in Chicago. There is a major cast or group Time Warping all the time in the Windy City. The first big theater for ROCKY was the Biograph, where it ran for eight years. There was also a rival cast at the Music Box Theater for a while.

The 400 Theater cast Midnight Madness in Chicago, 1989.

Columbia, Riff Raff and Magenta show their moves at the "400" in Chicago, 1989.

95

The Music Box Theatre and Absent Friends
present
A 69th Anniversary Celebration for

THE ROCKY HORROR PICTURE SHOW

Music Box celebrates 69th anniversary (69th week — that is).

Cast members on stage at Biograph in Chicago, 1978.

Dr. Frank-N-Furter lights up like Christmas tree in December of 1978 at Biograph in Chicago.

Voyeuristic Intentions — Biograph cast in 1985.

Today RHPS plays at the '400' Theater, which plans on breaking the Biograph's record. The '400' has already hosted two ROCKY HORROR Conventions, in 1988 and 1989. The latter had author Richard O'Brien as a special guest.

Chicago is a great 'ROCKY Town' and fans and cast members from elsewhere are always welcome.

The Rhode Island ROCKY Cast has been in existence for over twelve years, in nine different theaters. The cast, consisting of nearly thirty members, includes several persons whose activity in the RHPS cast dates back five years. Aside from performing the movie, the cast shows its enthusiasm for the movie by helping to raise money for leukemia research, participating in three major parades, and performing at local clubs.

Currently performing at the Meadowbrook Cinema, Warwick, the theater is in the midst of having the second longest consecutive run in Rhode Island.

Rhode Island ROCKY cast courtesy of Jay Brooks and Mark T. Weidner.

Photo: Russell Pedro

Photo: Russell Pedro

To combat the monotony that can be associated with the same people doing the show week after week, the cast regularly has "Virgin" cast nights, "Gender Switch" nights, where the guys play the girls' parts and vice versa, and "Theater Swap" nights, where the cast will switch theaters with another cast performing at a new cinema.

All the different names that the performing casts call themselves are usually clever take-offs on lines or lyrics from the movie. Some of them include: Double Feature, Transducer Players, Creatures of the Night and Voyeuristic Intention. The New York Cast never had a special title, we just call ourselves the 8th Street Playhouse Floor show.

In this section, I hope I can show you a good cross-section of theaters and casts from all over the country. They date from back to 1977 through today. Most come from my collection of all the photos I have received at the fan club. Unfortunately, this is not a complete group and my regrets to anyone still active who has not been included.

Neptune Theater, Seattle, Washington, 1978.

Photo: Gillian Gaar

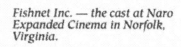

Fishnet Inc. — the cast at Naro Expanded Cinema in Norfolk, Virginia.

Courtesy of Fan Club Rep. Andrew Doyle.

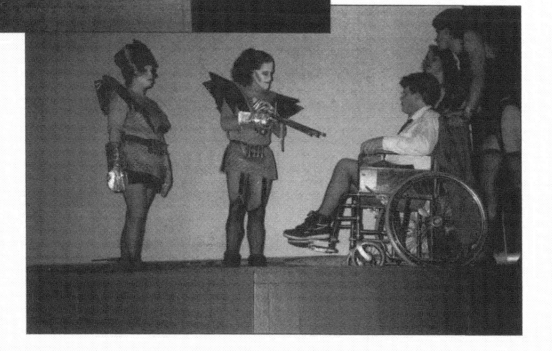

This is Voyeuristic Intention, the performance cast at the beautiful Rialto Theater in South Pasadena, California. Voyeuristic Intention has been doing the wild thing at the Rialto for going on ten years now. The two members with the longest term are Jeff and Shel Foss. (An interesting note—Jeff and Shel met at the Rialto, while in their Riff and Magenta costumes, and have been together ever since! They have now been married for three years, and have a family of four cats.)

*Neon Movies cast,
Dayton, Ohio.*

From: James Stiers

*The Players Group at the General Cinema in
Kitsap County, Washington.*

From: Unconventional Unconventionalist Keller Pilger

*Cosmic Vibrations of Daytona
Beach, Florida.*

Courtesy: Fan Club Rep. Loc Robertson

Photo: Edna Ott

Seduction Players of Mesquite, Texas.

From: Fan Club Rep. Miracle Tutor

Austin Riverside Twin — Austin, Texas 2nd anniversary.

Photo from: Danny Camacho

Jordan Bell and Saskatoon, Canada fans, 1989.

Loft Theater, Tucson, Arizona.

Photos courtesy: Fan Club Rep. Lawrence
Lasher (Dr. Scott)

𝕾𝖆𝖓𝖎𝖙𝖞 For Today are:

Brad Majors.....................T. Richard Cantrell
Janet Weiss.....................Diana Schroeder
Riff-Raff.........................Daniel Franklin
Magenta.........................Nichelle Ritter Jr.
Columbia.........................Marian Kelly
Frank N. Furter....David A. Leadbetter, Esq.
Rocky Horror......................Alexander Bozof
Eddie.............................Donald Davidson
Dr. Scott.........................Brock Sides, D.U.M.

Stage Management: Johnathan Gasquet
Lights: Kimberly Wells, Elizabeth Carr
Costumes: Wendimere Young
Make-up: Lynn Battistelli, Tonya Reese

Official Groupie Application

Name_____
Telephone Number_____
Cast Member Applying For_____
Gender (for filing purposes only)_____
Measurements_____
Preferred frequency of intercourse_____
Favorite Sexual Position(s)_____

Paste
Photo
Here

Please submit $5 application fee to T.Rick

Program from Raleigh Springs
Cinema Twin, Memphis, Tennessee.
House cast: Sanity For Today.

Dark Refrain (Fridays) and Lips Inc.
(Saturdays) of Capital City UA Theater,
Camp Hill, Pennsylvania.

From: Fan Club Rep. Jeff Young

Photo: C.E. Gramm

105

Balboa Cinema cast Newport Beach, California.

From: Fan Club Rep. Cindy Ashley

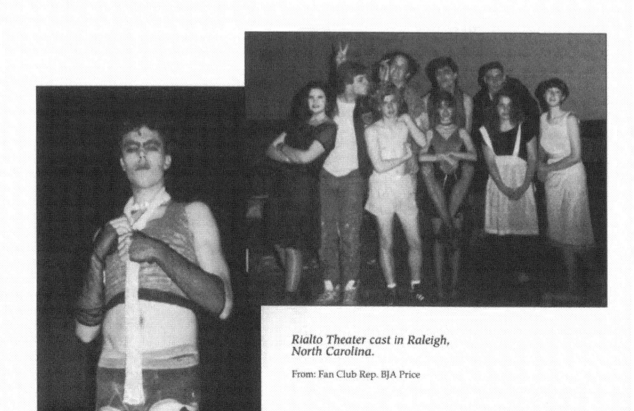

Rialto Theater cast in Raleigh, North Carolina.

From: Fan Club Rep. BJA Price

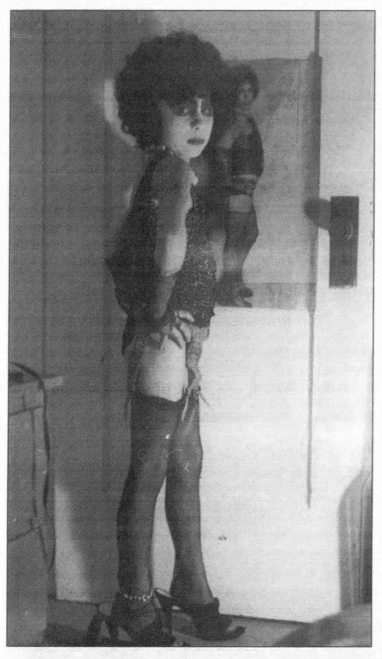

Judy Loftin as Magenta in Monroe, Louisiana.

An 8 year old Frank-N-Furter struts his stuff in Buffalo, 1979.

2nd anniversary costume contest of Forum in Atlanta, Georgia, in late 70's.

One of the most successful groups in the country, The Velvet Darkness, cast of the ABC Center Theater in Fremont, California, was organized by David Murdock.

Photos: David Murdock III (center right photo only) and Laurie Van-de-Werfhorst

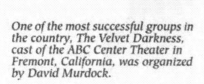

"Erotic Nightmares," cast of the Varsity Theater in Palo Alto, California.

Courtesy: Fan Club Rep. Melanie Garretts

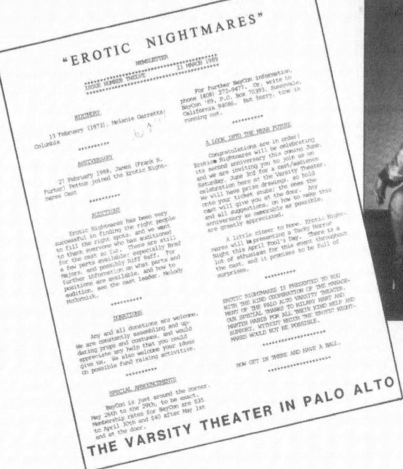

James Regan and friend of Berryton, Kansas. He was a big ROCKY fan who passed away of cancer (Rest In Peace).

Cape May Floorshow,
Cape May, N.J.

From: Joe Stevenson

Lori Dale and Kelly, Cuyahoga Falls, Ohio, 1986.

Costume contest at the Topeka Boulevard Cinema, Kansas, 1985.

King's Court Theater, Pittsburgh, Pennsylvania.

Courtesy: Fan Club Rep. Terry Thome

Photos: Ed Wivell

111

*C. Wallingford and company
in Indiana, 1983.*

Blue Skies Inc. performs in Florida.

Photos courtesy: Dianna Bennett

Cast members of Pensacola, Florida.

From: Fan Club Rep. Steven Earl Yoder (*Riff-Raff*)

Creatures Of The Night in Connecticut.

From: Gail and Joann Bertana

Baronet Theater, Canoga Park, California, 1984.

Members from assorted casts join forces at Alondra AM6 in Cerritos, California, 1989.

Sherman Oaks, California, 1984.

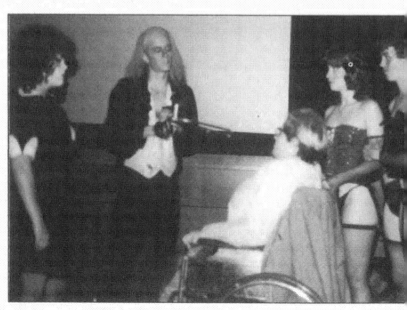

U. C. Berkeley, mid-80's.

Thousand Oaks, California, 1982.

The Ft. Lauderdale cast shows every week is "Spring Break."

Buffalo, New York cast, 1979.

Clinton Street Cabaret, Portland Oregon, 1987.

From: Fan Club Rep. Craig Williams

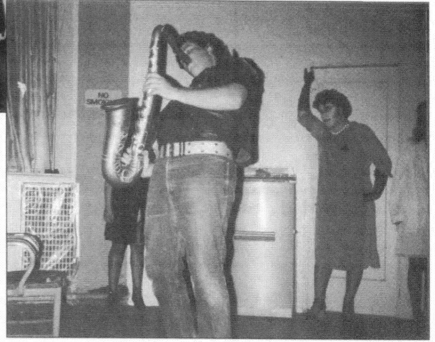

Another Dimension, Belmont Cinema, Belmont, California, 1986.

Photo from: Steve Lasky

"Dynamic Tension" of Soland CInema Six in California. This group started their own young artists performing company that became involved in fund-raising.

From: Fan Club Rep. Carol Filby

Erotic Nightmares, General Cinema,
Montclair, California.

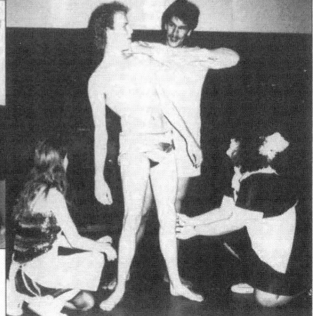

The Transducer Players of Harwan Theater, Mt. Ephraim,, N. J.

Photos: Boundry Studio

*Creatures Of The Night —
Melbourne, Florida cast, 1987.*

From: Fan Club Rep. Jim Millspaugh
(Eddie)

Julie Calabrese of New Rochelle, New York, 1979. Later on became long-running 8th Street "Frank."

"Denton Affair" of Santa Cruz, California make the cover!

ROCKY HORROR In England

British fan Honey McKinley.

Richard O'Brien and Sal meet with British fans.
(L. to R.) Paul and Gia Garner, Jon Richards,
Stephanie Monteith and Alison Foster.
Photo: David Freeman

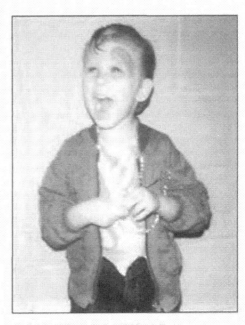

5 year old British fan Robert James
with "Eddie" scars.

The play of The ROCKY HORROR SHOW was very successful in England, but when the film was released in 1975, it was not a very big hit. The play was still running and the fans there were still devoted to the live show. The movie was released on video and was even shown on television. Since then, as stories of the audience participation in the United States began to trickle over, interest in the movie and its lore has increased. The video of the movie has been pulled from release and ROCKY thrives in many cinemas there, complete with cast and audience participation.

The most famous English group is "Charming Underclothes," who perform out of the Baker Street Cinema in London. This group was started by an American girl, Gia Millinovich, who was living there. She was originally a *Magenta*, but now she is the reigning *Frank-N-Furter*. Gia has married her *Riff Raff*, Paul Garner, artist extraordinaire, and together they put out a wonderful newsletter, "Dark Refrain."

Charming Underclothes cast of Baker St. Cinema in London.

Photos: David Freeman

Stephanie Monteith and David Freeman pose inside and outside of castle where movie was filmed at Oakley Court in England.

Photos: David Freeman

There is also a British fan club run by Stephanie Monteith. She and her fiance (married by this book's publication?), David Freeman, also perform with "Charming Underclothes," as Space *Riff* and Space *Magenta*. Stephanie and I are always in touch exchanging tidbits and info back and forth between the U.S. and the U.K. The address of their fan club is:

Time Warp
1 Elm Grove
Hildenborough, Tonbridge
Kent TN11 9HE
England

<u>ROCKY HORROR</u> In Other Countries

<u>ROCKY</u> fans crowd the front row in Finland.

Angie and Chris (both females) as Frank and Eddie in Munich, Germany, Nov., 1983.

Doors of <u>ROCKY HORROR</u> Theater in Munich painted as gates to Frank's castle.

Chris as Dr. Scott in Munich, Nov., 1983.

German ROCKY HORROR magazine.

ROCKY HORROR In Japan

The <u>ROCKY HORROR PICTURE SHOW</u> was released in Japan in the late 70's and was moderately successful. The only difference between Japan and the rest of the world was that audience participation had not officially reached the East. With the exception of a few import books and magazines and the <u>Audience Participation Album</u>, and, of course, those who experienced it while on vacation in the United States, most Japanese fans were unaware of this phenomenon.

Then in May of 1988, I received a phone call from a Japanese woman living in the United States who was representing a company in Japan that was going to bring <u>ROCKY HORROR</u> back to Japan in Tokyo and some other cities. Only this time they wanted to bring the film back, complete with audience participation. They wanted me to come and teach it to the fans. They asked me to bring three of my <u>ROCKY</u> cast with me.

I chose our present *Frank* at the 8th Street Playhouse, Barbara Boike and my sister Lillias who had been doing *Magenta* for over 10 years. Lillias is a wonderful singer who has performed live at conventions and <u>ROCKY HORROR</u> events, so we would be able to do some live numbers as part of our presentation. For *Riff Raff*, I chose a mutual friend of ours, Todd Rice, who was a fan but had never really played *Riff Raff*. Todd had two advantages, he could play the piano (in fact, his band played at the 10th anniversary) and he understood some Japanese!!! We had a month to teach Todd the role of *Riff* and get together a costume.

Sal speaks at opening night party for movie in Tokyo.

In July, the four of us flew to Japan, a little hesitant because we still did not know exactly what we were expected to do. After an extremely long flight, we were picked up at the airport in Tokyo and brought to our hotel in the city. That evening, we were taken to a restaurant to have a meal with a group of fans. Earlier, I had received a letter from a young woman named Julie who had inquired about the fan club and sent me some photos of her group of friends dressed as <u>ROCKY HORROR</u> characters. I had passed this on to the Japanese company and they contacted Julie and her friends, who were now to be part of our floor show.

Sal speaks to audience with interpreter at side.

Barbara performs in front of screen. Note English subtitles.

The first hour or two did not go well for us. Mr. Hiroshi, who brought me to Japan, expected me to teach them "English" responses to the film and participatory elements without the film?? Only a few spoke English. I did have a young girl who translated for me, but I felt ridiculous for it seemed to be a hopeless task and a total waste of time.

Finally, Mr. Hiroshi brought us over to the theater where <u>ROCKY HORROR</u> was to play. He put on the film and as if by magic everything began to fall into place. We assigned roles

---

Did you know — *the original plan for <u>RHPS</u> was to have the film in black and white until the scene in the movie when Dr. Frank-N-Furter throws off his cape?*

---

and these wonderful young people began to pick it up quite easily. The next night, I was amazed. It was our opening night in Tokyo. The word had spread and the cast came in full costume. Their performances were as if they had been doing it for years. They treated my three American cast members as big celebrities, especially after my sister sang "Science Fiction Double Feature" in a booming voice. My announcements were unusual that night, but fun, because as I did them I had a translator by my side. I had felt hesitant about going to Japan, but from that night on, the trip was pure pleasure.

Attack of the Japanese Magentas.

Japanese Brad and Janet (both females) perform. Note Japanese translation on side of screen.

Lines were shouted back to the screen in English and in Japanese. Todd delighted the audiences with some of his Japanese responses to the movie. We also did the show in the city of Nagoya and we had one day off to visit the old city of Kyoto. Those 10 days went by so quickly. We all felt like movie stars the way we were treated. ROCKY HORROR returned to Japan with a big bang. All subsequent performances were a sellout. There was lots of publicity about us and the Japanese cast in magazines, in newspapers, and on television. As we passed on the reins of <u>ROCKY HORROR</u> to the new Japanese cast, we returned to America.

Audience participation at Cinemarise Theater in Tokyo.

Japanese program from Sal's tour of Japan.

Tickets, passes, publicity materials for RHPS in Japan.

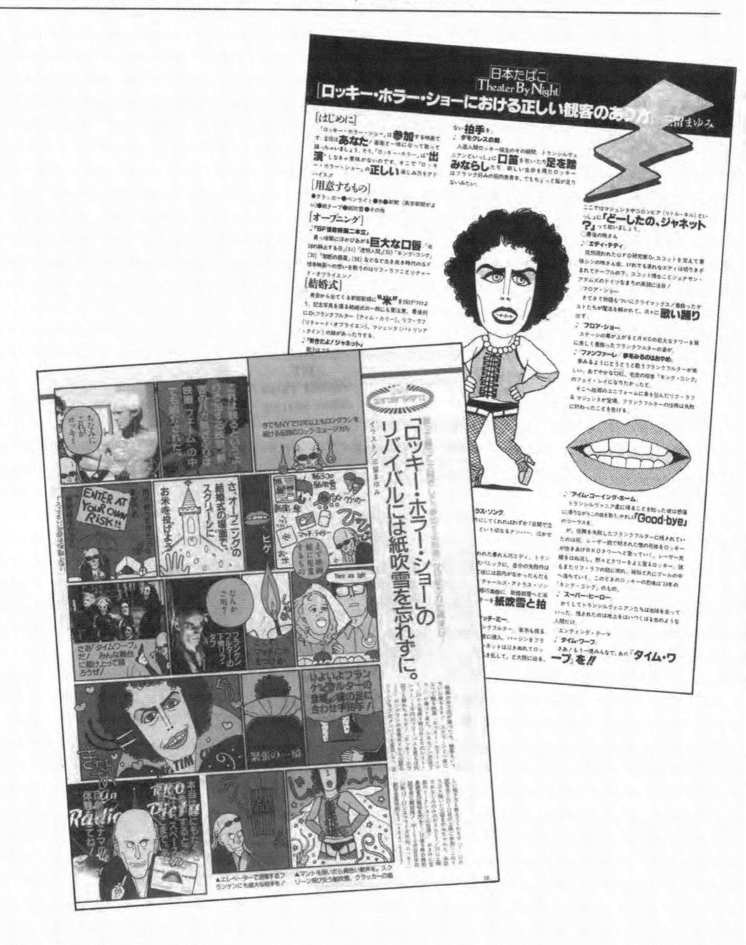

L aura Stein's one page newsletter at the Waverly Theater spawned the <u>Transylvanian</u> newsletter that later became a magazine. As far as I know, these were the first, but certainly not the only, fan-made magazines (fanzines). Over the last twelve years, I have received hundreds of issues of <u>ROCKY HORRO</u>R fanzines from all over the world.

These publications are sometimes hand printed or typed. They contain <u>RHPS</u> trivia, puzzles and information about a particular theater — its floor show cast and house rules. I contributed updates on the cult, the stars and new merchandise to many of these publications, usually in the form of a "Sal Says" column.

Some of the fanzines are printed and distributed free at the theaters; some are sold in the theaters at a nominal cost to help defray expenses; some have even been more ambitious and charge a modest subscription fee to cover costs and postage. Most importantly, these fanzines were and are the heart and soul of <u>ROCKY HORROR</u>.

The best and most successful of the fanzines was <u>Shoptalk</u>, which was begun in the early 80's out of Seal Beach, California, by Alan Hiero as a newsletter supplement to his "<u>ROCKY HORROR</u> Shop" (a mail-order business for various memorabilia). <u>Shoptalk</u> grew into a subscription publication with readers from all over the country.

In the mid-Eighties, Alan retired and gave the reins over to Betzi Vojtko, of Racine, Wisconsin, who carried <u>Shoptalk</u> on successfully until 1989. Betzi retired after the one-hundredth issue — a feat that will probably not be duplicated.

On the following pages are samples of the various newsletters, or fanzines, that have been enjoyed by thousands of fans over the years.

The very weird <u>Voyeur</u> — The Tri-State <u>ROCKY HORROR</u> Fanzine from Scott Johnson, Vineland, New Jersey.

The *ROCKY HORROR Newsletter* was
published in 1979 in Seattle, Washington.

THE ROCKY HORROR NEWSLETTER

ISSUE TWO JULY 1979

The Regulars. The
people who are as much a
part of the show as the

year, a special 3 p.m.
matinee showing of Rocky
Horror (without the noise
and antics of the mid-
night show) took place.
They not only originated
the concept, but with the
help of Special Event
Services they publicized
and planned the event
themselves. The group
also made news in a recent
Seattle Times article on
The Rocky Horror Cult.

For the Regulars,
costumes play an important
role. As David Fetrow put
it, "Once you've gone in
costume, you don't feel as
much a part of ot when you
go again out of costume."
At a recent Sci-Fi expo,
held in Seattle, a number
of the group's members won
prizes for their costumes.

While they admit that
they sometimes get tired
putting on the make-up,
they agree that they will
never tire of Rocky Horror
and The Time Warp.

One main theme
throughout Rocky Horror is
"Don't Dream It. Be It."
As Christine Fairley
spoke for the group by
saying, "We're being it."

NEW TIM CURRY ALBUM:

A&M Records has
released TIM CURRY's
second album. It's called
Fearless. This new record
is unique in that Tim
Curry wrote the lyrics to
six of the albums eight
songs. From the driving
"Right On The Money," to
the heartfelt and haunting
"S.O.S." Fearless show-
cases the creative
versatility of Tim Curry.

TRIVIA:

In 1975, TIM CURRY
appeared in both the
London and Broadway
productions of Tom
Stoppard's "Travesties,"
in the role of Tzara, a
Dadaist poet and sculptor.
The play went on to win
the coveted Tony Award as
Best Play of the Year.

To receive "The Rocky
Horror Newsletter" in the
mail, sign up for our
mailing list. You can
either sign up at Golden
Age Collectables in the
Pike Place Market (call
622-9799 for directions)
or call Special Event
Services 24 hours a day
at 522-9392 and leave your
name, address and phone
...... Subscription is

THE QUEENS COLLEGE
ROCKY HORROR FAN CLUB
NEWSLETTER

DECEM...
ISSU...

Time Warped — the first and only issue
of Queens College *RHPS* Fan Club.

Clinton Cabaret News from Portland, Oregon and Craig Williams,
Fan Club 'Rep.'

CLINTON CABARET NEWS
Volume 5 No. 1
Wednesday, November 9, 1988
This is a classified newsletter - NOT FOR PUBLIC DISTRIBUTION

C A B A R E T   D A T E L I N E

FRIDAY, NOVEMBER 11th - 5th Cabaret Meeting
SATURDAY, DECEMBER 3rd - Premiere of the 5th Cabaret

Organizational Meeting: Friday, November 11th 11:00 am at 4224 S.E.
Bybee Blvd, 775-5505.

OLD BUSINESS

1) Election of Officers
2) Cast Overview (Expansion/Lights)
3) Performance/Rehearsal/Lights)
4) Length of Cabaret

NEW BUSINESS

It is very important that ALL 5th Cabaret members attend. Nominations
received by premation is as follows. PRESIDENT: Craig L. Williams,
nominations accepted. DIRECTOR: Kerin E. Schultz - nomination accepted.
CHANCELLOR: Sharon Watson - nomination accepted. TREASURER: Steffani Plutner.
Williams - elected. TREASURER: Sharon Watson. SECRETARY: Craig L.
Simmons. Additional nominations will be accepted from the floor.

5th Cabaret Audition Meeting - Day 1

The first day of the 5th Cabaret Audition meeting of the CLINTON
STREET CABARET was held on Saturday, November 5th, 1988, at 1:15 P.M.
at the Clinton Street Theatre. The following members were present and
voting: John D. Simmons, Kerin E. Schultz, Steffani Lynn Plutner, Scott McMillan, Michael
Gwynne, Kerin E. Schultz, Dawn ..., Ken Short, Richard B. Abold, Craig L.
Williams, ..., Sue Davis, Sharon Watson, and Tiffany Laine. The
Fullname associate member was present and not-voting: Kathy Meinken.
President Craig L. Williams conducted the auditions.

11 members were present and voting out of 11.

1. FRANK-N-FURTER: John D. Simmons interviewed. 2/3 in elare emabled g.
   applicant. Vote was 11-0.

2. RIFF-RAFF: Michael Gwynne interviewed. He was the only
   applicant. Vote was 11-0.

3. EDDIE: Craig L. Williams interviewed. He was the only applicant.
   Karin. He was the only applicant. Interview conducted by
   abstentions.

4. CRIMINOLOGIST: Graham "David" Adams interviewed. She was the
   only applicant. Vote was 7-0 with 4 abstentions.
   Additional discussion. Vote was 9-0 with 10-1.

Fantasie Factory Players' Factory Outlet, 1987-1988.

From: Jeff Cisneros and Orlando, Florida cast

ROCKY HORROR Notebook hails from Camp Hill, Pa. featuring the Science Fiction Double Feature and Lips Inc. casts.

In 1980, William A. White published an excellent magazine, <u>The Hollywood Horror</u>, from Hollywood, Florida.

Your Favourite Obsession

Vol. 1, Issue 4   January 8, 1988

Merry new year! I don't know how many of you were at the Christmas show, but it was excellent! All of the cast was dressed up in their Christmas finery and showing their new Christmas underwear! We had a real proposal at the beginning of the movie. Amanda Dihrkoe, who usually plays Magenta, played Janet for this show, and her usual partner, Gerry Sturgill (Riff-Raff) played Brad for just one scene, the scene where Brad proposes to Janet, and Amanda got her engagement ring in front of the whole audience! She wasn't aware that this was going to happen, but she handled it beautifully. She only dropped her purse and flowers, not her lines! Congratulations to the happy couple!

Since Amanda played Janet, I was asked to play Magenta. I had worked hard on my lines and the cast helped me get to my spots. They were very patient with me and I want to thank them for their help. I learned how hard they work up there. We should let them know how much we appreciate their efforts in future! They ask for nothing but should get a standing ovation!

As you can tell by the banner at the top of the page, we have a winner for the "Name the newsletter" contest. Russ Pigg of Dayton, Ohio came up with it and I hope he is right. I hope you will make this newsletter and this movie your favorite obsession, as it is aim. Russ will receive a Rocky Horror Picture Show book "Telling all about the movie and a Dayton Movies T-shirt. Thanks, Russ! The cast is still looking for a winner for their "Name the cast" contest. They have had several entries, but no muscle. How about it, Dayton. Contact the Dayton Movies, 130 E. Fifth Street, Dayton, OH 45402. We also want to say a fond farewell to Scott Ricketts (Rocky) who will be putting on his last performance tonight.

In the January 3, 1988 Dayton Daily News, Art Snyder had an article on "What's Hot and what is Not" in Dayton for 1987. He erroneously decided that Rocky Horror Picture Show is one that is not, so he has been invited to join us at our showing tonight. We also want anyone who wishes to voice their opinion personally to write to Art Snyder, c/o Dayton Daily News, Fourth and Ludlow Streets, Dayton, OH 45402, and let him know that Rocky is ver-r-ry HOT!.

Recently, Sal Piro, the national fan club president, sent me a picture of Richard O'Brien, the author of Rocky Horror Picture dressed fit to kill! The caption on the back of the picture is "The Chic of R O'B." He certainly practices what he preaches! He was born in New Zealand, but went to England when he was a boy. He used Ritz O'Brien for awhile as a stage name. He has written quite a few stage plays and several have been made into movies. He is very versatile, writing dialogue, songs, acting in his works, and also putting out several rock songs in England. He was married to Kimi Wong, one of the Transylvanians, for awhile, but they have since gone their separate ways. He got his idea for "Don't dream it, be it" from a catalogue for Fredericks of Hollywood! He believes we should all be more tolerant of people who are different from us, and I agree entirely. If you have noticed, we have a wide variety of people who come to see Rocky, and I feel that all of them should be welcome, except for the inconsiderate people that try to ruin the movie for the rest of us.

Bye for now. Keep in touch. If you have any contributions, please contact me (after 5:00 P.M. please). Thanks.

Yours in Rocky, Carol A. Jenkins, editor. (Contributions by Erik A. Jenkins.)

<u>Your Favourite Obsession</u> was the newsletter of Dayton, Ohio cast edited by Carol A. Jenkins.

Hi everyone, we're glad to see you all here at the Amanda for the   Vol. 1 No. 5 most popular movie in N.Y., "The Rocky Horror Picture Show". Rocky has been playing here for over 145 nonsequitur showings with plenty more to come. We would like to Thank Bob Wilson for his creation of a new head for our newsletter "The Buffalo Rocky Review". It is an excellent piece of work that must have taken him "hours of labour"! Bob also is the mastermind behind "The Rocky Horror Comic Strip" and the various sketches which appear in the newsletter(like Magenta below). Geek. Jw more of Bob's work in the future!

"A Meeting With The Master"

Two lucky Buffalo Rocky Horror devotees are going to have their day with the master, Tim Curry. The article below, from this issue of Cream, tells their story. They are going to fly to New York for the realization of their dream, in the very near future. The two girls told us that right now Tim is visiting his home land in England, as soon as he gets back in the states they will have the long awaited meeting. They both have plenty of questions to ask our representatives here, and their interview will probably come up with some very interesting answers. Upon their return they have agreed to give us an exclusive interview as to what the master had to say and what happened. So stay tuned for the interview which will be in one of the upcoming newsletters. I think we all can agree that the 35¢ for the telegram was really well spent!

Reprinted from <u>Cream</u>

Jail was irrepressible: A writer from Cookers magazine in Buffalo wanted an interview with Tim Curry, who just couldn't find time to do it. Undaunted, she convinced Tim to call New York's own office checking for some time with the outrageous rocker. But alas, no go. "Did she say dial of course not! Geo lay, duh published Amanda's Horror and greeted with a shrug, begging for an interview, then Curry was informed of the request and how it was delivered, he decided to try to fit it into his busy schedule. He wanted to meet someone who would sing AND share a message for that kind of money...

<u>Buffalo ROCKY Review</u> from Buffalo, New York in the late 70's.

The very bizarre *ROCKY Review* came from the Ken Cinema in San Diego.

C. Wallingford in the early 80's gave us Lips, the Indiana Theater newsletter.

<u>ROCKY HORROR In Reno</u> was brought to us by Angie Whitworth.

The Transylvanian Monthly is brought to you by TWA — Time Warp Association of Atlanta, Georgia and Fan Club Rep. Dennis "Dinky" Knight.

Elin Winkler, Fan Club Rep. of San Antonio, Texas brings us The Fishnet Gazette.

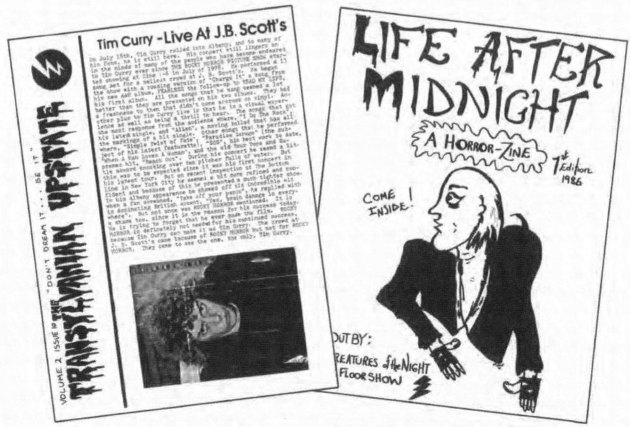

Transylvanian Upstate came from Albany, N.Y. in the late 70's.

Life After Midnight, published by Creatures Of The Night which toured many theaters in Connecticut.

In the mid 80's Eric Bradshaw of Rochester published _The Castle Times_ which had a minor feud with _Shoptalk_.

2nd issue of _ROCKY HORROR_ Shoptalk which was started by Alan Hiero of Seal Beach, California. This was the most successful of all _ROCKY HORROR_ fanzines. When Alan retired, it was ably taken over by Betzi Vutjko of Racine, Wisconsin. This fanzine ran over 8 years (100 issues).

The final and 100th issue of _ROCKY HORROR_ Shoptalk by Betzi Votjko.(Well done Betzi)

Midnight Madness comes from the cast of the Skywalk Cinema in Cincinnati, Ohio.

Rhode Island ROCKY was published by Dave Wasser in the late 70's.

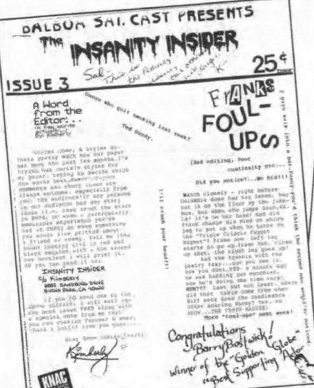

The Insanity Insider comes from the Landmark Balboa cast edited by Kimberly Heisner.

The Dossier is a newletter that comes out of Mt. Prospect, Illinois. This featured trivia quizzes from the "Bitchy" Rep. Dave Berry.

*Night Stalker from Bryon Howell
of North Haven, Connecticut.*

*Very well done one-time fanzine
Flash in 1979. Put together by
8th Street Playhouse "ROCKY"
Greg Kline.*

Lips Will Tell, the premiere fanzine to come out of Canada. Published by Katz a.k.a. Magenta.

Lips will tell...

The official Rocky newsletter in Montreal
Vol 2 #8: September issue $1

Registered trademark #223751A

Approved by Richard O'Brien

September issue
- Who the hell is Claude Rains? and Michael Rennie?
- the second cast in Mt. debate continues...
- Focus on: Eddie and Mike
- Life as understood with I/2 a brain
- & more!

THE TINTED ROSE

10 ¢

VOL. 1 NUM. 2

LET'S DO THE TIME WARP OLE!

This Saturday night a Spanish version of the Floor Show will
be done at the Graham, that Sweet Transvestite from Transexual
Tiajuana, and the rest of New York's most renowned floor show
will be there so come on up to the lab and see what's on the s...

Spanish rice at the wedding scene as well as formal dress w...
be optional.

NOTE: For this one showing only as an added treat, all wate...
used in the theatre's fountains will be imported from Guadale...

PUBLIC ANNOUNCEMENTS

Congratulations to everyone for abolishing the line
"PASS THE CRISIS". This week's "lucky and outdated"
line is: KIFF BERKOWITZ THE 44 CANDLE KILLER. Let's
kill this line once and for all.

A few other suggestions:

1- CERTAINLY NOT- This is one of the original lines
first used by a Rocky audience. I'm sorry to say
it hasn't been used much anymore. After the
criminologist says,"Spoil the events of the evening"
say- certainly not-

2- SAY IT- After Frankie says "Antici... if the
audience says "say it" at the same time, there
should should be a dramatic pause before Frankie
says "PATION". If done right,this can be very
effective.

We can all help to make Rocky the best as

LET'S DO IT!!!

The Tinted Rose came from the Graham Theater in Brooklyn in 1978. Many of this cast were with the original Waverly group.

---

the Denton Affair

M.A.L. FAN NEWSLETTER

October 1985

the `Affair` Begins

"The Denton Affair"
(Midnight Madness)
Movies At Lakeside Fan Newsletter

This is the first issue of "The
Denton Affair". We hope to be able to
put out one each month, but we can't
do it alone. We need your input. This
is your newsletter ! Make it what you
want it to be. If there are enough
letters, photos, etc. we could even
expand the newsletter. Please show us
your support. We're working for you !
Thank you
"The Denton Affair Staff

Send your questions, stories, photos,
etc. to:

"The Denton Affair"
31681 Hayes
Warren, MI 48093

This is a non-profit newsletter,
designed to give "Rocky" fans of
M.A.L. information and fun.

Editorial

A year ago I started getting involved with The Rocky Horror Picture
Show, at Movies At Lakeside. Back
then, (so long ago) audience attitude
and response was really bad. In April
1985, a live show, that I am proud to
be part of, popped up. Now, there is
more involvement. The theater is beginning to show a feeling of unity
and family. We still have a long way
to go, but we're making progress. All
of the participation is just part of
the fun. Please remember that the use
of props, yelling, dancing, etc. can
be taken away from us. Don't spoil
the fun for everyone.

Thank you to each and every "Rocky"
Horror" fan at Movies at Lakeside.

With absolute pleasure
Mike Hess

Toga - Toga - Toga

How many of you were at the 2nd
Annual Toga Party on October 16th?
The theater was pretty full, with a
large number of people dressed in
sheets. All different kinds of togas
could be seen, from the old Roman
style, revealing, traditional wear-a-
sheet style, to one that matched Dr
Frank N. Furter's surgical smock.

At the magical hour of midnight,
our fearless leader, Steve , the
manager, walked down the aisle in a
blue checked sheet, carrying two of
the prizes. He was accompanied by two
ushers, carrying a 100 lb. bag of
rice. The audience judged the togas
with applause.

3rd. Prize was shared by three
girls. They won a chocolate cake that
read "movies at Lakeside's 2nd Annual
Toga Party" and had the LIPS on it.

2nd. Prize was won by Tom Sliwa in
his "Charlie Brown" toga. He recieved
a copy of the Rocky Horror Picture
Show Audience Participation Album.

1st. Prize was won by Mike Hess as
Dr. Frank N. Furter in a green toga
with orange triangle. He won a 100 lb
bag of rice. When asked what he was
going to do with it he replied, "Why
bring it to "Rocky", and since a 10
lb. bag lasts me a month, I'll probably be bringing it to the 3rd Annual
Toga Party next year!"

Congratulations to all the winners!

Bring a Virgin!

Saturday, November 16th.
Bring A Virgin To Rocky Night !
The person with the largest cherry
brigade will win a special secret
prize!

Are you still a Virgin ? We'll pop
your cherry good on November 16th.!!!

In the mid-80's The Denton Affair came from the cast of Movies At Lakeside in Michigan. This was published by Mike Hess who now publishes Midnite Madness.

Midnite Madness calls itself the fanzine of the 90's. The latest endeavor of Mike Hess of the "Horrorable Hess" family. (For info. send s.a.s.e. to Transylvanian Museum, P.O. Box 292, Fraser, MI 48026)

The Master's Affair is the present successor to *Shoptalk* thanks to Tom Schaefer and company. (Send s.a.s.e. to: Master's Affair, 7605 Bristol Ln. Unit F, Hanover Park, IL 60103)

1st issue of Le Transylvanien, the magazine put out by fans in Paris.

Dark Refrains is an amazing fanzine that comes from Paul and Gia Garner of London, England.

Gothic News 2

The tour over the last few months has still been successful.

We went to Wimbledon where leaflets were handed out.

Security was the tightest ever seen. A thorough search was given.(even under my cap !) which i didn't mind,but no dancing was allowed,nor handing out of leaflets in the theatre.

One of our writers,Shelly,who is pregnant,wanted to sit in the bar through the show,but the manager wouldn't let her unless she bought a ticket!We still enjoyed ourselves though.

Only two cast changes. MARC SEYMOUR has taken over TONY MAYNE,who has had to pull out due to illness.We hope he gets well soon.

Finally,a special mention to the beautiful PHILLIPA BLAKE who was promoted to COLUMBIA from GHOUL just for Croydon.Everyone we spoke to said she was superb!

Dark Refrains

Dark Refrains is a new(ish) FANZINE from The Baker Street Group.

Costing 40p it offers 8 pages of pure Rocky,which to be quite frank (no pun intended) is absolutely brilliant.The articles are fresh,the news is up-to-date and the artwork is superb.

If you would like a copy of DARK REFRAINS contact Gia Milinovich at 33,Princess Road,London.

Gothic News comes from Jon Richards of Bournemouth, England.

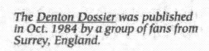

DENTON DOSSIER

BRITAIN'S PREMIER FANZINE OF

THE ROCKY HORROR PICTURE SHOW

SHOCK TREATMENT

AND

The Rocky horror show

SENSATIONAL
FIRST
ISSUE!

WITH FREE STAPLES

The Denton Dossier was published in Oct. 1984 by a group of fans from Surrey, England.

Time Warp 2

ROCKY HORROR FAN CLUB

© DAVID FREEMAN/ GE FOX

Time Warp is the magazine published by the British ROCKY HORROR Fan Club run by Stephanie Monteith and David Freeman.

Anjelica Huston accepting her mock Oscar at the 10th Anniversary celebration of the <u>ROCKY HORROR PICTURE SHOW</u>

Photo: Jean C. Pigozzi

MIKE HESS AND THE HORROR-BLE HESS FAMILY OF WARREN, MICHIGAN

Michael Hess became involved in ROCKY HORROR in 1984. In August of '85, Mike and his father Gary took over the computerizing of the Fan Club mailing list, which they still do to this day. Mike and his whole family attended the Tenth Anniversary in New York City in October of 1985. That November, Mike, his mother Diane and his sister Lisa formed "Shock Treatment," a local floor show at the Warren Cinema City in Warren, Michigan.

By July of '86, the group had thirty-five members, including performers, sponsors, and lights and sound workers. That same month, the floor show hosted Michigan's Five-State ROCKY HORROR Convention. When the group disbanded in 1987, Mike went back to his original theater, Movies at Lakeside, where he acted as emcee until 1989.

Mike has collected 2000 trivia questions concerning the movie, the play and the stars; he released 1800 of them in The Ultimate ROCKY HORROR Quiz book. He has also published information on ROCKY HORROR memorabilia in a collector's guide. Mike is the editor of Midnite Madness, a quarterly ROCKY HORROR fan magazine. He can be reached at:

The Transylvanian Museum
P.O. Box 292
Fraser, MI 48026

Note: The museum is not a place to visit. The name comes from the nickname for Mike's bedroom, which is filled with RHPS souvenirs.

Hoopla Mike and Family
Thanks For Your Work!

Mike Hess and Richard O'Brien at Chicago convention, 1989.

Lisa, Diane and Mike Hess at 10th anniversary.

ALAN HIERO

Alan Hiero (Emrich) discovered <u>ROCKY HORROR</u> in the late 1970's early in his college days in Long Beach, California. What he wanted after his first <u>ROCKY HORROR</u> weekend was a souvenir— button, t-shirt or something like that. There were none to be found. Distraught, he researched where, via mail order, souvenirs could be found. Soon, he acquired several of these trophies of fandom. His friends in line at <u>ROCKY HOR-ROR</u> soon asked where they could get them. Inspired by this "consumer demand," Alan opened his own <u>ROCKY HORROR</u> mail order business, The <u>ROCKY HORROR</u> Shop.

The "<u>ROCKY</u> Shop," as it was known, traveled around between the dozen or so theaters in the Southern California area, selling collectibles to the fans, and sponsoring a live floor show group, called Creatures of the Night. They garnered quite a good reputation for the perfection of their costumes, props and movie synchronization. Alan was one of their three *Frank-N-Furter* characters, but he more often managed than

Alan Hiero visits 'ROCKY' fans around the country.

performed. When his picture appeared, in costume, in the local newspaper, he changed his last name. Alan took on the name of Hiero after a run-in with his parents about "the good name of Emrich in the community." The new last name stuck and Alan Hiero is the name by which <u>ROCKY HORROR</u> fans around the country knew him.

Around the country? Yes, Alan reached out with his mail order business through the publication of a newsletter called <u>ROCKY HORROR</u> Shop Talk. This was certainly the most prolific, and arguably the best, <u>ROCKY HORROR</u> newsletter that ever saw the light of print. It became a labor of love and a vital form of communication linking its fiercely loyal readership. In effect, it became the ROCKY HORROR "family's" scrapbook.

The readers of Shop Talk formed a community of ROCKY HORROR fans with whom Alan visited one summer on what he deemed his "First Poor American Tour." Alan traveled far and wide that summer, visiting his readership and sharing stories with them.

Friendship was the currency of ROCKY HORROR in the early 1980's. When asked what was the one thing he'd gotten out of all his years of service to the ROCKY HORROR cult, Alan's emphatic answer was friends.

Well, some 400 showings later, Alan hung up his garterbelt and relinquished his ROCKY HORROR Shop business to Betzi Vojtko of Racine, Wisconsin. He gave away his collection of memorabilia as well (the "Shop Museum"), which included many treasures from both the movie and plays. He keeps one poster up in his home and also has retained his collection of foreign ROCKY HORROR Soundtracks. Also, Alan still has his costume tucked neatly away next to the photo scrapbook and videotape of those crazy days of his youth.

Hoopla Alan
The Spirit Lives On!

MICHELLE REHFELD

Michelle Rehfeld lives in Brooklyn, New York. She first saw RHPS at the end of the Waverly run. She became a regular with our New York group while we were in Queens in 1977, and she has been with us ever since. As of this writing, Michelle has seen the movie over 1,100 times and is one of the most dedicated fans I know.

Sal and Michelle Rehfeld at Eastside Cinema.

Back in the early days, when I was playing *Janet*, Michelle put together a gold lame dress to play *"Rocky"* as a goof to do the "Toucha-Toucha" number with me. Around the same time, we lost our *Rocky* and she temporarily moved into the role and then into it permanently. It was always a novelty having a female *Rocky*— but we had female *Franks* and male *Janets* and *Magentas*, we decided, so what was the big deal? Recently Michelle got together a perfect *Columbia* costume and now alternates between playing two roles.

Michelle has added so much to our theater, she corresponds with RHPS pen pals all over the world. She is a big Tim Curry fan and has seen all of his films, attending his past concerts and theatrical productions a number of times.

Hoopla Michelle
Keep Time Warpin'!

DENNIS MILLER

Dennis Miller, or "L.A. Dennis" as he is known to the fan club, has been involved with ROCKY HORROR for over seven years. He is the Los Angeles representative of the fan club and he holds the record for recruiting more members than anyone else. In fact, even when he travelled to Chicago for the convention in 1988, he spent half of the time going around recruiting new members.

Dennis Miller meets Tim Curry after performance of Me And My Girl, the musical that Tim toured in.

Dennis meets Dr. Demento at the Nuart.

Dennis is the M.C., *Riff-Raff* and resident ROCKY fanatic at the Nu-Art Theater in Los Angeles. Every year he organizes ROCKY casts to march in the annual Doo-Dah Parade in Pasadena.

Hoopla Dennis
Keep up the Good Work!

BETZI VOJTKO

After seeing the RHPS for the first time, Betzi went shopping for any information she could find; she found my name and the fan club address. Betzi wrote to me, sending poems and artwork which I sent on to Alan Hiero. Alan was impressed and contacted her about becoming a staff artist on Shoptalk, his RHPS newsletter. She continued to submit artwork and poetry until the summer of 1984, when Alan appointed her the new editor-in-chief. He was retiring in order to embark on a career in the strategy games business.

The home base of Shoptalk was now Racine, Wisconsin, where Betzi was ably assisted by her fellow "sleaze sister," Lory Kramer, whom she had met in 1983 at the Oriental Theater in Milwaukee.

When Alan asked her to take over Shoptalk, she couldn't imagine keeping it going for another five years. But she did!

All in all, Shoptalk's one hundred issues spanned a decade of decadence for hard-core ROCKY fans all over the world by being the longest-running international RHPS publication of all time. Shoptalk was a collection of everything of interest to fans — theater news, cast news, the stars' latest projects, artwork, poetry, photos of the film and fans, contributions from Richard O'Brien, pen pals, personals and timely editorials. Editorials were very important to Betzi. Many covered universal ROCKY problems (theaters, cast, parents, etc.) and others covered timely topics, such as Amnesty International. She devoted one whole issue to AIDS awareness.

Betzi identified with the character of *Magenta* and was instrumental, with her new found *Riff Raff* Gunning in forming The Celluloid Jam, the house cast at the Oriental Theater in Milwaukee in the fall of 1984. This group is one of the best known casts. They are recognized for their energetic performance, special celebrations and devotion to ROCKY HORROR. The entire cast came to New York for the 10th Anniversary, six of their members were finalists and three were winners in the costume contest, including Betzi and Rich in their "Space Costumes."

Betzi meets Wendy O. Williams of The Plasmatics who played Magenta in a stage production of ROCKY HORROR.

One of the highlights of Betzi's ROCKY years was performing on stage at the 10th Anniversary with the New York cast in front of Richard O'Brien and Patricia Quinn.

Betzi and Rich Gunning meet Pat Quinn at the 10th anniversary.

Betzi has now retired from <u>Shoptalk</u>, but her *Magenta* costume is always ready and her typewriter is always available.

Hoopla Betzi
Good Work!

THE COLLECTORS

Many fans around the country collect <u>RHPS</u> memorabilia. They have an unending thirst for knowledge and information that relates to <u>ROCKY HORROR</u> and the <u>ROCKY</u> Experience. Some of these fans have devoted years to the movie. They possess some of the most extensive collections in the country.

To name some of the collectors:

Jim Whittaker, II, Camp Hill, Pennsylvania

B.J. Owen, Portland, Oregon

Brian Himes, Indianapolis, Indiana

Mike Hess, Warren, Michigan

Bruce Cutter, Aurora, Illinois

Gene Chiovari, Chicago, Illinois

The one that I consider the "champ" is Danny Camacho of Austin, Texas.

Danny Camacho of Austin, Texas
and his ROCKY HORROR collection. (And this was 10 years ago!)

Bruce Cutter

Jim Whittaker exhibits his collection.

Epilogue

The THE ROCKY HORROR PICTURE SHOW has proven to be the most successful fan film in history — fifteen years of continuous showings in theaters around the world have never been equalled by any other movie!

As hundreds of thousands of devoted fans organized into fan clubs, theater groups and floor shows, the popularity of ROCKY HORROR continues to expand in the free world. As the Berlin Wall falls, ROCKY HORROR expands the experience to new horizons!

The future belongs to the ROCKY HORROR universe. . .

Also Available

The OFFICIAL ROCKY HORROR PICTURE SHOW AUDIENCE PAR-TIC-I-PATION GUIDE

by Sal Piro and Michael Hess

Binary PUBLICATIONS

Printed in Great Britain
by Amazon